Evangelizing Unchurched Children

A Pocketbook for Catechists

Therese M. Boucher

Resource Publications, Inc.
San Jose, California

D1167095

Reprint Department
Resource Publications, Inc.
160 E. Virginia Street #290
San Jose, CA 95112-5876
(408) 286-8505 (voice)
(408) 287-8748 (fax)

Library of Congress Cataloging-in-Publication Data
Boucher, Therese.
    Evangelizing unchurched children: a pocketbook for catechists / Therese M. Boucher.
       p. cm.
    ISBN 0-89390-496-1 (pbk.)
    1. Christian education of children. 2. Church work with children—Catholic Church. 3. Catholic Church—Education. I. Title.

BX926 .B68 2000
268'.432—dc21   00-038702

Printed in the United States of America.
00 01 02 03 04 | 5 4 3 2 1

Editorial director: Nick Wagner
Project coordinator: Mike Sagara
Copyeditor: Joanne Gregory
Illustrator: Timothy S. Boucher

Excerpts from the English translation of the *Catechism of the Catholic Church* for use in the United States of America Copyright © 1994 Libreria Editrice Vaticana—United States Catholic Conference, Inc. Used with permission.

Excerpts from the *General Directory for Catechesis* Copyright © 1997 Libreria Editrice Vaticana—United States Catholic Conference, Inc. Used with permission.

Excerpts from *Go and Make Disciples: Text, Study Guide & Implementation Process* Copyright 1993 United States Catholic Conference, Inc., Washington, DC. Used with permission. All rights reserved.

Unless marked otherwise, Scriptures are from the *Good News Bible with Deuterocanonicals / Apocrypha,* Today's English Version Copyright 1993, American Bible Society, New York. Used by permission.

Scripture quotations marked "NRSV" are taken from the New Revised Standard Version of the Bible, copyrighted, 1989 by the Division of Christian Education of the National Council of the Churches of Christ in the United States of America, and are used by permission. All rights reserved.

Parts of Chapter One, including "The Church Jumps for Joy" on page 11, appeared as articles in *The Catechist* (March 1999) and is being used with the permission of the publisher, Peter Li Educational Group, 330 Progress Rd., Dayton, OH 45449.

Story on page 23 courtesy of Mary Keesee. Used by permission.

Prayer on page 48 courtesy of Red Cloud Indian School, Inc. Used by permission.

To My Dad, Harry Fenner

Contents

Introduction 1

Chapter One
What to Do When God Isn't Home 3
    The Spiritual Side of Life
    Consecrated in Baptism
    A Closer Look at Evangelization
    The Religious Background of the Family
    Recipe for Sharing

Chapter Two
Meet Jesus, Jesus, and More of Jesus 13
    Jesus Is Our Alpha and Omega
    Jesus, the Master Catechist
    Jesus Is Present
    Sacramental Encounters with Jesus

Chapter Three
What's the Whole Story Here? 23
    The Catechist's Faith Story
    Handing On Kernels of Truth
    Use of Literary Arts to Announce the Good News
    The Message Is Eternal

Chapter Four
The Drama of the Scriptures Comes to Life 33
    Voice of God and Breath of the Spirit
    Scripture As the Church's Book
    The Drama of the Bible
    Promoting Gospel Values

Chapter Five
Playing with the Church's Symbols 43
    What We See, Touch, Hear and Feel Can Build Faith
    Faith Is Uttered through Symbols
    Visual Arts As a Language for Exploring the Spiritual
    Formula for Using a Symbol to Teach

Chapter Six
What More Can an Evangelist Do? 53
    Essential Moments of Evangelization
    Build Disciples and a Culture of Belief
    Evangelizing beyond Class Time
    Radical Dependence on the Spirit
    Catechists As Prophets of an Evangelistic Vision

Glossary of Terms 65

Introduction

It was a cloudy Tuesday morning in Lent when I met my first unchurched child. Weekday Mass was over, and I was looking forward to a few minutes of prayer in the quiet, old brick church. I had just settled back in the pew when seven-year-old Billy wandered in from the bus stop. The boy ambled into the semi-darkness and tapped me on the shoulder. "Say, what is this place?" he asked in a loud voice.

"It's a church," I whispered.

"Is that so? What's a church?" he wanted to know.

I had never been faced with such a striking question, so I rummaged though the answers I had learned in religion class many years ago. None of them seemed to fit, so I just shrugged my shoulders, but my hesitation didn't phase him. Billy set off down the center aisle to find out for himself. I caught up with him just inches away from the tabernacle.

"What's that candle doing in the jar? Do you get a lot of wind in here?"

I could see by now that this fellow wasn't going to leave without some answers, and whispering was definitely out.

"The candle is like a sign in a window that says Jesus is here."

"Here in this building? You're kidding!" he said as he quickly surveyed the whole room in astonishment.

"No, I'm not. He's sort of in the gold box next to the candle." It was the best I could do under duress.

"How did they catch him and get him in there?" he wanted to know.

I thought to myself, "I certainly had never caught him, at least not for very long. Who could? Well, of course he doesn't fit in there. How could something be so ridiculous and so true at the same time?" I was baffled. But my new friend was undaunted. We continued down the side aisle at warp speed and managed to cover all the high points, even the "confessional," but that's another story.

I have met many, many unchurched children since then. There was the little girl who thought "forgive us our trespasses" meant "don't walk on the grass" and the boy who liked to play alligator by crawling from pew to pew on his stomach. There was the teenager at St. Patrick's Cathedral in New York City during the historic visit of St. Thérèse's relics. She wanted to know what was in the Plexiglas-covered wooden box in front of the altar, so I took a deep breath, smiled, and gave it my best shot. Then there's my dad, who began walking to Mass by himself before the age of seven. He heard about Jesus from his Protestant Uncle Eddie as they sang country music and hymns on the back porch.

If you are a catechist, you have already met many "unchurched children."* Studies based on work done by Gallup and the Paulist National Catholic Evangelization Association tell us that less than 50 percent of those adults who identify themselves as Catholics are active churchgoers. These inactive Catholics are defined as people who go to Sunday liturgies less than twice in six months, not counting Christmas, Easter, weddings, and funerals. When I told a friend who's a Director of Religious Education that I was working on a book about unchurched children, she stopped in mid-thought and replied, "Oh, you don't mean just kids in the catechumenate. You mean most of the children in my program." She's right. Although no formal studies have been done, a growing majority (between 50 percent and 70 percent) of the children in religious education programs come from families of inactive Catholics.

This book is not about why these children and their families are inactive or unchurched. It is important for catechists to let go of the idea that this situation is someone's "fault" or that it means we have failed. This book explores new and hopeful guidelines offered by the church's *General Directory for Catechesis*. God's love for unchurched children is unfailing. Catechists can develop a sensitivity to this love and to the spiritual needs of these children. Each chapter offers practical ways to grow in this sensitivity. The Catechist's Prayer section offers a way to talk to God about being such a catechist. The Checklist for the Aspiring Evangelist section helps you think through an evangelistic approach to faith and to teaching. The Books, Websites and Resources section offers a wide variety of ways to learn more (updated resources will be available at the author's website www.christkey.com). The Something to Try section is a sample lesson that puts the ideas in each chapter into practice. God may be shared in many ways with these children as they wonder what's in the box, what's in the tabernacle, and what's in their own hearts. God has invited them into your class and will help you reach them.

---

* For the purposes of this book, I am using the term "children" to talk about boys and girls between the ages of five and twelve. I have avoided the term "young people" because there is no commonly accepted definition of this term. I am also using the phrase "inactive Catholic" and "unchurched" interchangeably in regard to children. Because these children are one generation after their inactive parents, most of them have the experience of being unchurched. Besides, the last thing that comes to mind when describing children is the word inactive. See the glossary for more precise definitions.

Chapter One

What to Do When God Isn't Home

One Tuesday ten-year-old Jimmy came to my office as a part of his preparation for first communion. He had learning problems in school but experienced no difficulties when it came to prayer. Jimmy explained that his grandmother had given him a cross for his bedroom, "So I just stare at him and tell him everything. Now that Grandpa has lung cancer, I ask Jesus to help my parents stop smoking. They could die, you know. And I want them to come to church on Sundays too, but they don't want to."

Every catechist has a Jimmy or even a half dozen Jimmys in his or her class. At teachers' meetings there is often a quiet discouragement about the lack of religion in homes and the lack of family attendance at Sunday liturgies. One catechist said she felt as though she was teaching Chinese. Another had questions about what material was basic enough for students like this. Sometimes there's a wide gulf between what is covered in a catechist's textbook and what can be understood and accomplished with children who have a weak religious foundation.

The monumental needs of many of today's children challenge us to reexamine catechetical assumptions and retool as catechists. The *General Directory for Catechesis*, written by the Congregation of the Clergy and published by the United States Catholic Conference, offers a comprehensive and insightful look at the goals, assumptions, and methods involved in reaching hundreds of Jimmys. It is meant to give universal guidelines for the church. The document reminds us that "the aim of catechetical activity consists in precisely this: to encourage a living, explicit and fruitful profession of faith" (66; see CCC 1229; CD 14). We know this and we try. But we are also part of a broader effort called evangelization. This means that somehow catechists must be part of "the process by which the Church, moved by the Spirit, proclaims and spreads the Gospel" (48). The directory offers a blueprint for adopting an evangelistic outlook on teaching children. This does not mean that catechists are expected to convert youngsters and whole families, or that inactive families are without faith. It does not mean that each catechist must be holy in a way that is beyond anyone's wildest expectations. What is called for is a shift in thinking and a greater awareness of how the Spirit may be working. The goal of this pocketbook is to explore such a promising new vision and to generate some practical suggestions for catechists. The Gospel may be translated in many exciting ways into lessons that are sensitive to children's needs for evangelization without coming across as either foreign or irrelevant.

The Spiritual Side of Life

Catechists have an advantage in the way children look at life. Children are curious, multisensory, and holistic in their approach to reality. Teachers can offer all sorts of stories, insights, and experiences that will be examined both at face value and often with an eye toward a deeper significance. Even when children may not seem as though they are paying close attention, they are searching out what is real and true and beautiful. Even though materialism or a false sophistication may make some of them jaded, they are always on the lookout for something genuine. Children are in the process of piecing together a mosaic that will become the "big picture" for them. We as church can respond to these hungers with a faith that is itself "whole," that is "rooted in human experience," and that "gives light to the whole of existence and dialogues with culture" (GDC 87).

I once worked with a confirmation candidate who had not attended any religious education sessions except for vacation Bible school when he was about nine years old. It had been a positive experience that opened up the whole world of Scripture and Gospel stories. For several years, whenever he faced minor problems, Keith turned to God by reading the Bible. When he was in high school, Keith found out he had a serious hormone disorder. This condition was a major blow to his self-image and raised issues of acceptance by peers. On one particularly bad day, a friend told Keith about an upcoming confirmation retreat. Keith begged his mother to let him go. The session he attended was a mixed blessing. He learned more about God but also felt awkward with the others in his group. The big breakthrough for Keith happened when he joined a parish clown troupe as part of a service project. He discovered a new freedom in being "odd" and a real ability to identify with Jesus in his willingness to face adversity to proclaim the kingdom of God.

Consecrated in Baptism

The majority of the children in our programs also have the advantage of the sacrament of baptism. Parents and godparents have already asked for "faith," and God has responded. Jesus is present to them. They have been named and recognized by God and are already immersed in the waters of God's life. St. Catherine of Siena (Italy 1347–1380) says it this way, "the [Christian] is in God and God in the [Christian] just as the fish is in the sea and the sea in the fish" (*Wisdom of the Saints* 204). The *General Directory for Catechesis* reminds us that the catechumenate is the model for all catechesis (59). It is important for us to view a child's preparations for baptism, confirmation, and Eucharist as a whole. Catechists are involved in stirring the waters of baptism or digging wells to get at the springs of new life that are just beyond the surface. Catechists are like Jesus, who taught by the Sea of Galilee. We, too, gather children at the shores of the river of life.

Any and all instruction is meant to be part of an ongoing formation process, a journey toward faith. For children, it is as if the whole process of Christian initiation (entering the church and the life of Christ through baptism, confirmation, and Eucharist) is in slow motion. The journey also has very noticeable bumps, false starts, and even breakthroughs. Catechists are like guides who point toward the main road in order to "nurture the roots of faith." Catechists are also like artists, given a year to offer part of "an apprenticeship [in] the entire Christian life" (GDC 67). It is a humbling task that often catapults teachers back to the roots and foundation of their own faith. Sometimes catechists find that their own hearts get caught up in the same important "process or ... journey of following the Christ of the Gospel in the Spirit towards the Father" (143). As a catechist, you may also experience getting lost, forgetting your destination, and losing all sorts of provisions along the way.

A Closer Look at Evangelization

Today's children are in need of a compass and a map for the journey toward faith. They may live in an atmosphere of weakened Christian values. "The first victims of the spiritual and cultural crisis ... are the young" (181). This situation calls for a new evangelization. Catechists seek to make the presence of God explicit in a variety of ways. Catechists are involved in both proclaiming the message and offering opportunities for spiritual formation. "The heart of catechesis is the explicit proposal of Christ to the young man in the Gospel" (183; cf. Mt 19:16–22). Catechists offer invitations to follow Jesus. Use Jesus as your compass, your anchor. Jesus is the way. As one young girl declared after her first experience with the sacrament of reconciliation, "I have to have a plan to straighten things out with Jennifer so I can see Jesus better."

Evangelization also involves an invitation to "come and see." As both a catechist and an evangelist, you are like Paul, who pointed out the statue to the unknown god. When your own personal response to God is real, no matter how feeble, you become a witness to God's presence. This invitation to faith is also built on your ability to visualize God's particular love for each of your children. Being able to do this is a way of realizing the truth expressed in Romans 8:38–39. "For I am certain that nothing can separate us from [God's] love: neither death nor life, … neither the present nor the future … there is nothing in all creation that will ever be able to separate us from the love of God which is ours through Christ Jesus our Lord." This conviction is what your children will find most intriguing.

The Religious Background of the Family

It is not easy to believe in God's love as you become more aware of the meager religious practices of your children. Some are like the movie character who was home alone, except that they sometimes live in a spiritual void. Some are like spiritual travelers looking for a home, but all that they find are locked doors. You may ask yourself, "How can I prepare them for the next step in faith or the next sacrament when so much about the last one seems to be lost or hidden?" Start by acknowledging the fact that children are products of a family's faith, and it is only natural for children and families to struggle with faith. Remember, there is no such thing as a family that does not provide a religious education. Each parent, guardian, or sibling has painted a portrait of a personal God or gods. Catechists can neither deny nor replace what has been learned. What we can do is offer a broader glimpse of the church's experience of God. We can act on the belief that every family is offered a gift and "that Christ will make his home in [their] hearts" (Eph 3:17). Then we must step aside and trust God.

An important point offered in the *General Directory for Catechesis* is that parents are often in need of "evangelistic nourishment." Their desire to let God into their children's lives often reflects their own spiritual needs. We must keep in mind that when "inactive" parents bring their children to us, it is somehow an act of faith. Often our contacts with these parents can provide breakthroughs or "essential moments" for those who are "nonbelievers and those who live in religious indifference … who need to complete or modify their [own] initiation" (49). God can intervene at any moment.

Children are often members of whole spiritual communities in need of hearing the Gospel without condemnation.

Catechists must be aware of the quality of their relationships with such families. Parent notices, phone calls, invitations, and even the way you talk about family life can have an effect. Catechists can become a resource for information and even web-based adult learning. Catechists are a link to whatever the parish offers in adult faith formation. They can also be a sign of the family's acceptance by the whole community. For example, one parish asked each child in its program to make a candle for the church's birthday on Pentecost. All the candles (each one was six by three inches) were mounted on banners and carried in a procession. Many parents were touched by this gesture and searched out their child's candle after Mass.

Even when a catechist is fairly certain that children are part of "inactive" or "unchurched" families, he or she can express confidence in God's personal love for whole families and refer to the gifts that a child's parents asked for during baptism. Catechists can teach children how to give their families to God in prayer. You can also help children make connections with members of their extended family who have a lively, personal experience of God. An overwhelming majority of children see their grandparents or an aunt and uncle as models of faith. You can also use examples and stories that acknowledge how hard it is to believe in God and to follow Jesus. Catechists can introduce the saints, who are always willing to be spiritual aunts and uncles. There is much a catechist can do once he or she accepts the spiritual conditions and needs of whole families.

Recipe for Sharing

The catechist's task is "to help a [young] person to encounter God, which … means to emphasize above all the relationship that the person has with God so that he [or she] can make it his [or her] own and allow himself [or herself] to be guided by God" (139). It isn't a question of saying or doing more than what is already included in a good lesson plan. Most of us don't need a new recipe in order to proclaim the Good News. It isn't a question of sharing Christmas greetings such as ".com all ye faithful" or offering opportunities to e-mail nursing home residents, although many new possibilities are on the horizon.

Evangelizing catechesis is more like letting the dawn stream through a room that has been lit by only a small lamp. Catechists offer an invitation to healing and wholeness in the fullest sense of both words, an invitation that is born of a vital passion for letting God into their own hearts and showing others how to find the doors to their hearts. The motto of the church's efforts to celebrate the third millennium is, "Open wide the doors of your hearts to Christ." The Italian words first used in this quotation from Pope John Paul II's installation exhort us to "Blow the doors of your hearts off their hinges."

Your own baptism and immersion into God involve a call to proclaim Jesus. The personal invitation to know Jesus Christ and to share what you know are the true moving forces of catechetical activity, which is "to proclaim him, to 'evangelize,' and to lead others to the 'yes' of faith in Jesus Christ" (*Catechism of the Catholic Church* 429; cf. GDC 231). That call may not have occurred in the most inspiring or glamorous circumstances, but you are connected with the children in your charge through a common baptism. They are brothers and sisters in Jesus Christ despite their weakened spiritual conditions. Even though these youngsters may look more like a collection of aliens on a starship than a gathering of fledgling disciples, God is with you. You can grow with them. Have confidence that a gentle introduction to Jesus, the Scriptures, liturgical prayer, communal symbols, and the life of the church will be enlivened by the Spirit of the one who raised Jesus from the dead (cf. Eph 1:15–20).

Remember, one of the goals of catechesis with unchurched children is to present portraits of Jesus as invitations to conversion. Conversion can happen at any age from early childhood through the elder years. Keep in mind that many types of conversion can tumble out on top of each other. Conversion can be spiritual (a falling in love with God), intellectual (understanding God), moral (living Gospel values in relationships), ecclesial (bonding with the Body of Christ), and socio-political (translating the Gospel into actions that touch our whole world). Each person (adult or child) also has a certain style or pace for conversion. Some move quickly and others slowly. Any one of these types of conversion can come first or last. One young man carried a Bible in his briefcase for five years before he began to read it. He read bits and pieces for another three years until he was finally ready to talk to someone about what Jesus meant to him.

Catechist's Prayer

The prophet Isaiah tells us that God's word is like snow and rain watering the earth, making crops grow, and providing food for us (Is 55:10–13). Use the following prayer each week as you plan your lesson. Keep a list of your students' names in front of you.

God, may the words that I speak to your children be like snow and rain. Help me speak about your love. Help me be an instrument of your abiding presence. Show yourself to each one of them in whatever way you choose. I bring each one into your presence now. Lord Jesus be with _____. Jesus, our redeemer, touch _____. Jesus, prince of peace, come to _____. *(Take the time to picture Jesus standing beside each one. Conclude by thanking God for each child by name.)* Thank you for using me to bless your children. Help me persevere as a faithful witness. Amen.

Saints Who Knew How

St. Thérèse of Lisieux entered a cloistered convent at age fifteen and became an assistant novice director at twenty. Within a convent of twenty-five, she was responsible for the spiritual formation and education of five sisters. Four were older than she was, and two were relatives. Her guiding principle in working with these young sisters was an unwavering confidence in God's love for them:

> Our Lord doesn't need to make use of books or teachers in the instruction of souls; isn't he himself the Teacher of Teachers, conveying knowledge with never a word spoken? For myself, I never heard the sound of his voice, but I know that he dwells within me all the time, guiding me and inspiring me whenever I do or say anything. A light, of which I'd caught no glimmer before, comes to me at the very moment when it's needed (*Praying with Thérèse of Lisieux* 103).

Checklist For The Aspiring Evangelist

The *Catechism of the Catholic Church* calls baptism the gateway to life (1213). Here are a few ways to appreciate your own invitation to live the Good News and to share God's love in a vibrant way with others.

☐ When and where I was baptized _____

_____

☐ How I first heard about Jesus _____

_____

☐ Something I really believe about God _____

_____

☐ How the baptismal light of Christ shines through me _____

_____

☐ Why I am glad that I was baptized _____

_____

☐ My image of Jesus at a joyful moment in his life _____

_____

When the disciples returned from sharing the Good News in neighboring villages, Jesus was so happy at their success that he literally jumped for joy (according to the Greek text of Lk 10:21–22). Did you know that the word "rejoice" appears seventy-two times in the New Testament and that the word "joy" appears sixty times? Paul exhorts us to rejoice in the Lord always (Phil 4:4). This is a remarkable and important element of being a catechist.

Books, Websites, And Resources

Adels, Jill Haak. *Wisdom of the Saints: An Anthology*. New York: Oxford University Press, 1987.

Ghezzi, Bert. *Keeping Your Kids Catholic*. Ann Arbor, Mich.: Servant, 1989. A collection of articles with many practical suggestions for parents.

Heffernan, Anne Eileen. *Fifty-seven Saints*. Boston: Pauline Books and Media, 1995. A collection of easy-to-understand biographies. See *www.pauline.org*

Knox, Ronald, trans. *Autobiography of St. Thérèse of Lisieux*. New York: P. J. Kennedy and Sons, 1958.

Schmidt, Joseph F. *Praying with Thérèse of Lisieux*. Winona, Minn.: Saint Mary's Press, 1992.

www.nccbuscc.org — The United States Catholic Conference offers evangelization resources such as *General Directory for Catechesis* by the Congregation for the Clergy, *Guide for Catechists* by the Congregation for the Evangelization of Peoples, *On Evangelization in the Modern World* by Pope Paul VI, *Catechism of the Catholic Church* translated for the United States of America, and *Because We are Disciples* (a video presentation). The website gives daily Scripture readings. They can also be reached at 800-235-8722.

www.rpinet.com — Resource Publications, Inc., offers an extensive number of links to a wide variety of resources—catechetical, liturgical, storytelling, parish ministry and clip art.

"Holy Traders" — plastic coated cards that include many contemporary saints. Call 800-242-8467 or visit their website at *www.holytraders.com*

Many of the books at the end of chapters can be obtained through the publishers or through *www.amazon.com* or *www.bibliofind.com*, which locates out-of-print books.

Something to Try: "The Church Jumps for Joy"

The Easter Vigil is the high point of the church year, and we, as church, use one of our most treasured prayers called the Exsultet to say yes to who Jesus is for us. "In the joy of this night" we bring out one of our most vibrant symbols, the large paschal candle. The presider invites everyone to "let the place resound with joy" as he holds up the light of Christ in the center aisle of our darkened churches.

As catechists it is important to enter into the joy behind this exuberant prayer and to have an appreciation for the light that we hold so dear. You and I must lift up and celebrate the flame and the energy that Jesus brings to help us "dispel all darkness." Catechists who can convey the joy of the Easter Vigil are proclaiming the very foundation of the Easter message itself, the centerpiece of all evangelization. There are ways to present the excitement of the Easter Vigil in classroom prayer.

1. Use a paschal candle to demonstrate both its markings and symbols and the Easter realities that we hold so dear. Point out the alpha and omega which are the first and last letters of the Greek alphabet. These letters tell us that Jesus is the source of all good things. He is also our destiny and greatest treasure. Point out the cross with the five red spots that represent the wounds of Jesus. They are like marks of courage and selflessness in his determination to bring new life. Point out the place for the current year on the candle. The Easter Vigil prayers give us a chance to offer the whole year to God. Every Sunday thereafter we are reminded of the light of Christ shining throughout the year for us.

2. Children are intrigued by the mystery of darkness and all the creatures that can roam our sullied imaginations. "Goosebumps" books and monster stories are their stock in trade. Talk about being in a dark place with no electricity for a long time. Some have probably experienced power failures, being lost in the dark, or feeling a deep loneliness in bed late at night. What would anyone alone or lost in the dark think and feel when help and light arrive?

3. Darken the classroom and light a large candle. Pray a simplified version of the Exsultet. If the children are in middle school or above, they can hold tapers while you pray together. They could also renew baptismal promises after this prayer. Ask the group to repeat the response after each section of the Exsultet, "Yes. Yes! Amen. Alleluia!"

Rejoice, every heavenly angel and all the stars in the universe. Jesus Christ, our king is risen. R.

Rejoice, you dirt and water. Rejoice, every plant and animal. Jesus has brought light and glory. R.

Rejoice every Christian, every parish, every pew. Let this place resound and shine with joy. R.

Rejoice, anyone who has done wrong. Jesus has washed us clean. Death and sin are broken forever. R.

Run, everything that is evil or hateful. We are strong now.
We are saved and unafraid. We are made whole by Jesus. R.

Yes. We want the Easter light. We choose Jesus, our Morning Star. We want this fire in our hearts. R.

Chapter Two

Meet Jesus, Jesus, And More Of Jesus

The Moms and Tots group met weekly in the church basement. Some of the eighteen families represented were active members of the parish, but most were not. We offered these preschoolers seasonal introductions to faith. Because it wasn't Lent or Advent, I decided to teach body prayers by using a large cross with an ascending Jesus. My first surprise was that most of the preschoolers had never seen a crucifix before. They wanted to know who Jesus was and why he was trying to fly. I gave a brief explanation and then let them take turns touching Jesus. We played a game that involved pointing to different body parts on Jesus and on our own bodies. Then we ended with a song. All the children wanted to touch Jesus one more time before they left. My second surprise was that one little girl kissed him good-bye, and all the rest followed suit. One mom had tears in her eyes as Jesus and I left the room.

Jesus Is Our Alpha and Omega

There are many ways that Jesus can be a part of catechetical sessions at every level of faith. The first way is hinted at in the scriptural title "Alpha and Omega" found in Revelation 22:13. Jesus is the beginning and the end, the overall point of reference and the goal for what is taught. The *Catechism of the Catholic Church* says it this way: "'At the heart of catechesis we find, in essence, a Person, the Person of Jesus of Nazareth …' (*Catechesi tradendae* 5). To catechize is 'to reveal in the Person of Christ, the whole of God's eternal design reaching fulfillment in that Person' (CT 5)" (426). Jesus is the goal of each session in some way and the goal of each year's program. St. Ambrose (Italy 340–397), who was elected Bishop of Milan while he was a catechumen preparing for the sacrament of baptism, said: "When we speak about wisdom, we are speaking of Christ. When we speak about justice, we are speaking of Christ. When we speak about truth and life and redemption, we are speaking of Christ" (*Wisdom of the Saints* 14).

The GDC describes Jesus as the "foundation ... of catechesis: ... the center from which all other elements are structured and illuminated" (41). It is important to keep Jesus in focus as we present all sorts of material from textbooks. This focus becomes even more important with children who have never met Jesus or heard much about him. Catechists may also face cultural stereotypes of Jesus, which will take their proper places as a fuller and more faith-filled picture emerges. The simplest way to keep Jesus in sight as the goal of catechesis is to imagine that you are introducing *all* the children in your session to Jesus. Ask yourself, "What would someone know about Jesus from being in this class today? How did we add to the big picture of who Jesus is for us?" Think of yourself as building a large mosaic that is pieced together week by week and prayer by prayer. Such a mosaic takes shape through pictures, Scriptures, film clips, discussion, faith sharing, and even reflective silence.

Jesus, the Master Catechist

John's Gospel refers to Jesus as "the way, the truth, and the life" (14:6). This is a reassuring title for catechists. It means that you are actually team-teaching with Jesus. All of his teaching methods, abilities to reach people, and healing miracles can be a part of your sessions. Jesus the teacher, the sower of seeds, is standing right beside you (see GDC 138). The pressure is off, and all those prayers of desperate frustration are heard. You are not alone. The God who has called you to teach will empower you. God is with you and will inspire you. Jesus will send the Holy Spirit as you plan lessons and when you are searching for just the right example, the right words. The Holy Spirit, who is the primary agent of evangelization, will act through you and in the hearts of your young people.

Jesus is also a master teacher because of the methods that he uses to explain the kingdom of God. He teaches with everyday objects. He mixes dirt and spit and Spirit to heal a man. He uses stories and parables to awaken religious imagination. He quotes and embraces the Hebrew Scriptures. He issues invitations and welcomes questions. Jesus has a real compassion for the different ways his disciples need to learn. He is willing to show Thomas the holes in his side or to meet with Nicodemus at night. And most of all, Jesus empties himself to become all the more involved with us. He is also willing to help your children "see" with their hands, voices, movements, and bodies.

Catechists can also take an incarnational approach that employs a broad range of art forms throughout the year—literary arts (written pieces such as stories and poems), performing arts (such as skits), and visual arts (such as drawings). Catechists can awaken all the senses at every step in a lesson. During this motivation you play with a lesson's theme and related human experiences. During the presentation of content you can include concrete examples and descriptions. Activities and prayer experiences can help children apply lessons in a sensory fashion. Considering and creating art helps children focus and opens the way for self-reflection and prayer. The literary arts can help children hear God on many levels and jog them into conversations with God. Performing arts can help youngsters "put on the new self, which is created in God's likeness" (Eph 4:24). Techniques such as mime, puppetry, skits, processions, and masked drama help children act out the message. Visual arts become doorways to understanding and pointers for applying what is learned. Through all of these art forms children can experiment with religious symbols and images on their own level. St. Bernard of Clairvaux (France, 1090–1153) said, "Jesus is honey in the mouth, melody in the ear, a cry of gladness in the heart" ("The Name of Jesus"). In other words, meeting Jesus is a multisensory affair.

Jesus Is Present

An important part of what catechists do is hinted at in the title "Emmanuel," God-is-with-us. Catechetical sessions can be like labs for realizing the many ways that Jesus is present in daily life. Paul's letter to the Romans reminds us that it is not a question of *bringing* Jesus into the world, the classroom, or our lives. "God's message is near you, on your lips and in your heart" (Ro 10:8). The word of God has become flesh, our flesh, and is as close as a heartbeat. An awareness of the presence of Jesus is the foundation for helping children build a relationship with God. "'The definitive aim of catechesis is to put people not only in touch, but also in communion and intimacy, with Jesus Christ' (*Catechesi tradendae* 5). All evangelizing activity is understood as promoting communion with Jesus Christ" (GDC 80).

The first step in offering this awareness to unchurched children is letting them "eavesdrop" on your own growing relationship with Jesus. The experience of teaching can be an opportunity to fall in love with God on a new level. Let yourself be "evangelized" alongside your students. There is always more of Jesus. It takes humility to admit that you need to hear about Jesus over and over again. As Paul VI said, the church (that's us) "has a constant need of being evangelized, if she wishes to retain freshness, vigor and strength in order to proclaim the Gospel" (*On Evangelization in the Modern World* 15). Invite Jesus into your class long before it even happens. Start by talking to him about your students' needs and about the good things you see in them.

If personal prayer is something new, begin by finding a quiet place. Do what helps you see and hear Jesus in your mind's eye. Use a song, a prayer, or a picture. Then imagine your classroom and watch Jesus enter. What do you see him doing? What does he say? It is also important to talk to God about the other areas of your life. Many catechists who are new at having a regular prayer time experience a flood of emotions, memories, obstacles, and personal issues when they approach God in this way. This is perfectly normal. Give yourself time to learn how to come before God. Consider praying more often and for about fifteen minutes at first. Try starting off with the daily readings or a few paragraphs from a spiritual book. Find a friend with whom to share prayer experiences. Consider St. Thérèse of Lisieux's definition of prayer and choose to persevere.

> Prayer means launching out of the heart towards God. It means lifting up one's eyes, quite simply, to heaven, a cry of grateful love, from the crest of joy or the trough of despair. It's a vast, supernatural force which opens out my heart, and binds me close to Jesus (*Praying with Thérèse of Lisieux* 80).

Spending time with God before we teach is encouraging and also becomes a foundation for prayer during class time. Your confidence in God's presence will be contagious. Jesus is with us, each of us, during catechetical sessions. Textbooks stress prayer because it is a way to acknowledge the presence of God in the lives of children. One goal of prayer is to provide the space and privacy that children need to talk to God. Just the silence and bodily stillness that is part of prayer become a doorway to God for many children. Another goal is to help them develop an ability to focus on Jesus. A third goal is to bring families, pets, issues at school, and the whole world before God.

Some catechists help children focus by using physical objects such as an enthroned Bible, a prayer corner with mats, or a candle. Some catechists use a meditation process that begins with everyday objects. The *In My Heart Room* books by Mary Terese Donze, ASC, provide examples of meditations for children. Another catechist uses a plastic globe and a box of Band-Aids. Each week the children put a Band-Aid on the parts of the globe that need Jesus most. There are many, many possibilities. The point is that Jesus is with you, and part of your job is to let the children take a peek at Jesus, even if they can only watch you pray at first.

Sacramental Encounters with Jesus

Jesus is the resurrection, the new Adam, the bread of life, and the good shepherd. Many of these titles reflect what happens during sacramental encounters with Jesus. Some catechists are involved in immediate preparations for these encounters, but all of us can nurture children's experiences of the sacraments they have already received. It is important to talk about sacraments as ongoing ways to keep meeting Jesus. "Communion with Jesus Christ leads to the celebration of his salvific presence in the sacraments" (GDC 85). Catechists can foster and model active participation in the church as a way to meet Jesus together. The foundation for a strong liturgical education is laid when the sacraments are seen as a communal treasure hunt.

Teachers can also familiarize children with liturgical gestures, prayers, and one-liners, thereby connecting liturgical prayer with everyday life. When someone shares bad news say, "Lord have mercy" or "Peace be with you." My favorite is "God bless you." (Have you noticed that many people who use this as a response to a sneeze are now leaving out the word "God"? Let's keep it!) Happy occasions provide even more possibilities for liturgical exclamations—"Thanks be to God!" or "Alleluia!" Parts of the liturgy and even the priest's prayer gestures can be used during prayer times with the children, so that if and when unchurched children get to the sacramental celebrations, they will recognize familiar elements.

Of course, it can be frustrating to invite unchurched children to celebrate the sacraments because sacramental worship seems like an unattainable goal for them. Even though God's love is freely given, catechists face what looks like a negative response to that love. We may feel like telephone solicitors who sense indifference, or even agitation, on the other end of the line. Remember, catechists are not salespeople, and Jesus and the church are not products. "The Christian faith is, above all, conversion to Jesus Christ (cf. *Ad Gentes* 13a), full and sincere adherence to his person and the decision to walk in his footsteps (cf. *Catechesi Tradendae* 56)" (GDC 53). You *cannot* condemn a family's spiritual decisions, but you *can* equip children to make their own decisions somewhere down the road. You can offer an awareness of God's ongoing invitation.

One of the first retreats I experienced was about following Jesus. One speaker compared a life of discipleship to a family's decision to emigrate to America. They saved money for passage and had just a little left over to buy cheese sandwiches for the long ocean voyage. Halfway through their long trek the children got bored and went exploring. Just minutes later they burst into the family cabin with armfuls of fresh fruit and meat, potatoes, and even a few sweets. The parents were appalled and accused their children of stealing from rich passengers. "No, no!" the oldest boy declared. "The food is free. It is a part of the trip!"

There is hope for parents. Welcoming or enrollment rites adapted from the Rite of Christian Initiation of Adults can be used as a way to welcome both child and family into a sacramental preparation process. During these rites parents present their children as candidates for a sacrament like Eucharist. They are asked if they will help with the child's preparations. If these rites are respectful and affirm parents, then we are giving them the support they may need to look at their own faith. Remember that the church is meant to be a communion of saints, a web of sustaining relationships. It may take only one heartfelt invitation for someone to walk through the church doors. I have met parents who became Catholic in order to celebrate first communion with their children. I have met fathers who wanted to be confirmed with their sons and mothers who were baptized with their babies. This certainly doesn't happen in most cases, but catechists should be aware of the possibilities.

Sacramental preparation can become not only a teachable moment but also an "essential moment" of evangelization for both children and parents. The vicarious experience of a young person's preparation for sacraments can be a springboard for parents. Because many adults are living lives of religious indifference, catechists must be aware of some parents' need "to complete or modify their [own] initiation" (GDC 49). Catechists can send home a welcome packet with information about the parish and about sacramental preparation for adults. Some parishes also provide some form of hospitality and informal sharing during children's sessions or assistance in forming car pools. Others have a team of "first communion" parents who visit other parents. It is up to us as parish communities to dream up ways to invite whole families to the sacraments. Once you have done your best, you must then step back. Success can not be measured in numbers but in the willingness to reflect Jesus, who is among us.

Catechist's Prayer

St. John Perboyre, CM, was one of the earliest missionaries to China. He lived from 1802 to 1840 and belonged to the Vincentians. His prayer can help you become aware of your body language as you teach and as you lead children in prayer.

Oh my divine savior, transform me into yourself.
May my hands be the hands of Jesus.
May my tongue be the tongue of Jesus.
Grant that every faculty of my body may serve only to
glorify you ...
Grant that I may live but in you and by you and for you
That I may truly say with Saint Paul: "I live now, not I,
but Christ lives in me" (*Praise Him!* 83).

Saints Who Knew How

Francis De Sales (1567–1622) lived in France during the time of the Protestant Reformation. At one time he did something very unusual by teaching a deaf man and preparing him for first communion. Francis wanted to reconcile Calvinists with the church. No one would listen, so he left hand-written copies of his sermons on people's doorsteps. He spent time with the village children. His kindness to the children led to the conversion of forty thousand people.

Francis was the first person to give spiritual direction to ordinary people, especially through letters and through his book called *Invitation to the Devout Life*. The book was controversial because of its everyday images and the use of jokes. He describes believers as lovers who "can never stop thinking about [Jesus], longing for him, speaking about him. If they could, they would engrave the name of Jesus on the hearts of all humankind" like lovers carving initials in a tree. One of his jokes is "To be an angel in prayer and a beast in one's relations with people is to go lame on both legs."

☑ Checklist For
The Aspiring Evangelist

It is good to get in touch with your own understanding of Jesus and to explore the wealth of images we value together as a church. Fill in the blanks to get your bearings as a disciple.

☐ When I close my eyes and try to picture Jesus, I see _____

_____

☐ An event in the life of Jesus that I can identify with is _____

_____

☐ More than anything, I wish Jesus would _____

_____

☐ A place where I experience the presence of God is _____

☐ If I could ask Jesus to explain one thing it would be _____

☐ One way that Jesus is present in my students' lives is _____

☐ A place in my classroom where Jesus might sit or stand is

Following are some of the titles for Jesus in Scripture. Underline a favorite or two. Circle one or two that are troublesome for you. Repeat a title slowly as a way to begin your own personal prayer time.

Emmanuel   Chosen One
Lamb of God   Prince of Peace
Son of David   Suffering Servant
Good Shepherd   King
Living Bread   Savior
Son of Mary   Christ
Healer   Messiah
Lord   Bridegroom
Just One   Word of God
Light of the World   Redeemer
Image of the Invisible God

Books, Websites, And Resources

Adels, Jill Haak. *Wisdom of the Saints: An Anthology.* New York: Oxford University Press, 1987.

Donze, Mary Terese. *In My Heart Room* and *In My Heart Room: Book Two.* Liguori, Mo.: Liguori Publications, 1982 and 1990. These offer meditations.

McBride, Alfred. *Images of Jesus.* Cincinnati: St. Anthony Messenger Press, 1993. Develops ten images (titles) as ways to grow in intimacy with God.

Rosage, David E. *Rekindle Your Love for Jesus.* Ann Arbor, Mich.: Servant Publications, 1996. Presents reflection questions that Jesus asked his disciples.

Scanlon, Michael. *Title of Jesus.* Steubenville, Ohio: Franciscan University Press, 1990. A brief collection of titles and their backgrounds.

Schmidt, Joseph F. *Praying with Thérèse of Lisieux.* Winona, Minn.: Saint Mary's Press, 1992.

Storey, William G., ed. *Praise Him!* Notre Dame, Ind.: Ave Maria Press, 1973.

Zannoni, Arthur E. *Jesus of the Gospels.* Cincinnati: St. Anthony Messenger Press, 1997. Presents a scriptural and scholarly explanation of Jesus.

For short biographies of saints try *saints.catholic.org/* A number of American saints' shrines can be visited by your class on the internet.

www.setonshrine.org
www.cabrinishrineny.org
www.littleflower.org
www.katherinedrexel.org
www.stjohnneumann.org
www.stjudeshrine.org
www.solanuscasey.org

www.stbenedictsfarm.org/19frs2.htm "The Name of Jesus, A Sermon on the Song of Songs."

Something to Try: "Meeting Jesus in Prayer"

Part of prayer is picturing Jesus so we can begin to speak with him. Some people look at a crucifix, a stained glass window, or a picture while they pray. Some older people use "holy cards" or illustrations in a prayer book. Try collecting several large pictures of Jesus and use them for a silent voting exercise. Invite children to choose two pictures and write one good quality for each choice on a slip of paper. Tabulate the results and discuss what the children like and dislike about some of the pictures. A European picture of a pale, thin Jesus might make him look weak. A bleeding Jesus might lead to a discussion of the plague during the Middle Ages. The goal is discovering the many ways we know Jesus.

Generate a list of names for Jesus and use them to write a litany. Point out some of these names in the children's religion books or in Scripture. Share why a particular name was used. Dim the lights and use both the pictures and litany to speak to Jesus aloud together.

Jesus, the Good Shepherd,
Come be with me.
Jesus, my savior, my brother,
Come be with me.
Prince of Peace, Bread of Life,
Come be with me.
Jesus, Jesus, you are with me.

Chapter Three
What's The Whole Story Here?

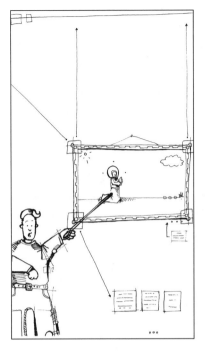

People become catechists for a variety of reasons. Here's Mary Keesee's story.

I was a full time office manager for a law firm, president of a charitable organization, wife, mother, daughter, and career woman. I was overdoing it and according to my friends, I was too responsible. I literally never relaxed and often felt unbalanced. Then my husband had a heart attack followed by quadruple bypass surgery. It triggered a realization inside me that life is too short to be too busy. I had to make a series of life style changes. I quit my job even though I was scared about money.

In the fall when our pastor asked for help with religious education, I wasn't too busy so I signed up. At first I was uneasy about teaching. I wasn't even sure I could carry on a conversation with six-year-olds. But my students and me, we muddled through. And I stayed with the class into the second level. After that I was hooked. Watching them receive Eucharist brings overwhelming feelings of joy, and real hope that they will grow in their spiritual life. Certainly, my spiritual life is changing. The lessons I am now teaching my classes have become lessons for me. I deal with life differently. I try to recall a lesson Jesus taught us. Then I truly learn in my heart and in my head. God gives me strength.

It is common for catechists to learn along with the children they teach. When the lessons, prayers, and Scriptures are taken to heart, they become stepping stones for personal growth and faith. Many catechists experience new levels of God's presence in their lives, either as a source of consolation or as a challenge to conversion. This is good. It means catechists can convey a "living awareness" (GDC 107) of faith and its struggles.

Children are keenly aware of what catechists believe and are most affected by the witness of catechists (cf. 141), the story of a teacher's own relationship with God. Children know how much of a part Jesus plays in your life. Therefore, getting in touch with your own faith stories is important. "No methodology … can dispense with the person of the catechist …. The charism … given by the Spirit, a solid spirituality and transparent witness of life, constitutes the soul of every method" (156).

The Catechist's Faith Story

Humans are story animals, and catechists are no exception. We all use stories to process what has happened to us, whether it is an earth-shattering event such as a collision on the highway or just the trivial details of the day. As a catechist you share faith stories with spiritual meaning. You give concrete evidence that Jesus can be an important character in the events of every human being's life. This doesn't mean that every faith story is worthy of becoming a Hollywood script. It does mean watching for God in daily life. If unearthing personal faith stories is an unfamiliar task, then start by collecting faith stories from other believers and saints. Put a line or two from a saint's story into a spiritual diary of your own and describe some of your reactions to the story.

Another starting point for generating a faith story is to list events for which you are grateful. Choose one item on the list, such as the birth of a child. Thank God for all the pleasant details associated with the event, and then let the unpleasant details emerge. Picture Jesus at the event and imagine his response or help. After you have finished rethinking this memory, write a short paragraph about it in your diary. St. Frances Cabrini exhorts us, "Let us warm our hearts with holy gratitude, which in turn will inebriate us little by little with divine love" (*Travels of Mother Frances Xavier Cabrini* 192). After you are accustomed to this kind of reflection, you can also give God painful memories. Start by describing the difficult feelings to Jesus. Imagine what he would do to help. Then thank God for what you have discovered about this difficulty.

A diary of your experiences will help you discover patterns in your life. Brett Hoover has a good description of these patterns in his book about losing your religion. "Our spiritual journeys are not random jaunts through the back roads of life …. For each of us, God is hatching a plan, a spiritual itinerary not unlike the auto club's famous 'trip-tik.' The plan grows as you grow. It is your life-long task to cooperate with God in developing and uncovering [this] plan" (16). If you would like to take some time to look at God's presence through your whole life, I recommend *Discovering My Expe-*

rience of God by Frank DeSiano, CSP, and Kenneth Boyack, CSP. This book will give you a head start on journaling.

Sharing faith-filled episodes in your life accomplishes several things. First it offers children a living example of what is taught and gives unchurched children a concrete grasp of what you and I mean by "faith." When faith sharing goes hand-in-hand with the material in a lesson, children discover a lively vision of the faith-filled life. Faith sharing teaches children that revelation is about ongoing dialogue with God. When a catechist shares what it is like to trust God or to love the unlovable, for example, these things seem more possible. Examples may sound strange to unchurched children but will strengthen the development of their religious imagination and religious vocabulary. One priest used a fake cell phone to "interrupt" himself while he was teaching about prayer. Then he shared his own difficulty with praying near a phone and how challenging it is for all of us to pay attention to God.

Handing On Kernels of Truth

Some catechists feel uneasy when it comes to such a personal definition of faith sharing and evangelization. Unresolved issues in their relationships with God seem like obstacles to this approach. Some catechists worry about being foolish or out of sync with the world that children represent. Some struggle with inadequate religious backgrounds of their own. Some aren't aware of God's activity in their lives. There is good news for all these situations. A willingness to teach means that God has already intervened in your life in some way. Now, both gifts and limits can become a part of growing in faith. St. Elizabeth Seton taught hundreds of children about God but agonized over her son's spiritual condition. St. John Bosco rescued thousands of homeless boys but struggled with acceptance from his peers. It is possible and helpful to share your struggles, as long as you share a resolve to stick with God until you get answers.

As a catechist, you must investigate the core of your life's story, your theme song, or a common spiritual thread. You need to examine what it means for you to believe in God. Look for ways in which the "Story of Stories" intersects with your own life. Ask yourself what your baptismal vows or the scriptural proclamation that "Jesus Christ is Lord" or the tenets of the Nicene Creed mean for you. Practice stating these beliefs out loud. If you have difficulty with these tasks, get the kind of support you need to grow. One of the wisdoms of the *General Directory for Catechesis* and the *Catechism of the Catholic Church* is the insight that the Creed is a pillar, or support, for what we believe as catechists. In practical terms, you can actually add "creedal" statements to your lesson. You can say, "I believe in Jesus," or "I know God made the heavens and the earth." Such statements give the unchurched young person a glimpse of the backbone of your faith.

You have a faith the size of a mustard seed and the opportunity to share that faith in some small but powerful way. That sharing or "witnessing" will bring life in ways you may not immediately see. In the early '90s people in my part of the country were excited about a rare opportunity to see a space shuttle fly by. That morning I scurried off toward a farmer's cornfield where a dozen eager people watched the sky. I had misjudged the distance and didn't arrive in time to see the shuttle. What I did see was just as impressive. The sight of the shuttle touched and moved the twelve spectators in a dramatic way. Some jumped. Some pointed. Some waved and shouted, "Hello!" All of them cheered in unison and began to chatter about their experiences. These examples of "witnessing" were profound and inspiring. Witnessing is a gift that makes faith contagious. When catechists have the courage to share the living word, God brings healing and hope.

Use of Literary Arts to Announce The Good News

Many religion books incorporate faith stories that become examples for the main points in a lesson. Storytelling is an old standby for catechists. A story allows children to relive an event or an emotion that is no longer dependent on time or place. Canonized saints and fictitious characters become heroes in faith stories. As children identify with them, their insights become like theme songs in the search for God. Catechists can use many literary art forms in addition to simple storytelling to uncover the presence of God in our midst. You can help children play with the meaning of words through all kinds of poetry. You can help children verbalize their own inner stories through writing recipes for faith, newspaper articles, commercials, litanies, webpages, e-mails, prayers, fairy tales, song lyrics, and journals. You can use word mapping, which starts by circling an important word and then drawing branches or rays for other associated words. For example, the tree of life connects us to images of the Garden of Eden, the cross of Jesus, colorful autumn foliage, or a rope swing in the backyard.

No matter what a child's background may be, he or she needs to process the big and important things that touch lives, such as love, death, forgiveness, and world peace. Stories help children discover universal connections between our world and God. Good stories have a power that makes them prophetic and ablaze with the fire of the Holy Spirit.

One of my favorite examples of a prophetic story is *The Boy Who Could Sing Pictures* by Seymour Leichman (Doubleday, 1968). It is about Ben, the son of a court jester, who felt compassion for the poor and wanted to give them more than a few minutes of juggling and jokes. Ben saw a great sadness in these poor people. He didn't know what else to do, so he sang.

> He sang about the land, and the doves, and the rainbow about the sun. As he sang the doves appeared and the people saw them. They could see in the air above them everything that he sang ... and the sadness was gone. And so it was in each town .... The images poured out. Emeralds and golden crowns and laughing children. Roses and lilacs, and angels hung on the horizon .... Word of him spread like wind.

A literary piece that carries the weight of God awakens dreams from deep within and invites children into new worlds, new experiments with faith. The main character in a story can personify the issues that children face. Stories can introduce new kinds of heroes and role models. It is up to you as a catechist to offer stories in a meaningful way. Here are some of the elements for telling a story:

1. Master the text and fall in love with the characters.

2. Convey an event. (A story moves.)

3. Heighten the action and the emotion by using a prop, a gesture, and an assortment of voices.

4. Repeat a line so that it becomes a refrain.

5. Use the children's names in the story.

6. Vary the pace and volume.

7. Take time after the telling to talk to the children about what happened, but remember that some stories take us to holy places and evoke an initial silence.

8. Help children get in touch with the inner dialogue that a story triggers in their hearts and minds.

Because the church invites us to participate in a new evangelization (GDC 58), it is important to tell stories that announce the Good News in explicit ways. Such stories can be vehicles for reaching families—in letters that are sent home, as part of parent meetings, and during welcoming or enrollment rites and large prayer services. Children and families need a whole inner library of faith stories as a reference. Catechists can connect the Good News to current events and public figures so that children can apply the Good News to the world around them. An example of living the Good

News in public is Tara Lipinski. She considers her St. Thérèse of Lisieux medal to be as important as her Olympic gold medal for skating.

Another example is John Glenn, who traveled in space both as a young man and as an elderly person. You might print a worksheet that asks parents what it was like when they were young to hear about astronauts flying into space. Parents and children could then share what it would be like to fly in a space shuttle today. Ask them to read the following statement by John Glenn and write a thank-you litany about the universe.

> To look up at this kind of creation out here and not believe in God is to me impossible .... I wish there were words to describe what it's like to look out the window from up here and see a 4,000-mile swath of Earth go by under us (quoted by Earl Lane, "Glenn Is Awestruck and Needle-Struck," *Newsday* [2 Nov 1998]: A06).

Catechists can also help children discover the religious history behind some secularized holidays such as Hallow's Eve, Christmas, and Easter. One catechist invented a play about Father Nick, who became St. Nicholas and then Santa Claus. A seamstress kept adding costume items to Father Nick's black garb to make him more believable. After each item was added, she asked Father Nick or Bishop Nick if the addition was okay. His stock answer was, "It's okay as long as we love Jesus." Such imaginary treatment of history helps children develop a global religious imagination and gives them the strength to adopt countercultural values.

The Message Is Eternal

Unchurched children need to know that God will be an active character throughout their entire lives. A catechist who is preparing children for sacraments should share stories about children and teens finding Jesus in the sacraments months and years into the future. Jesus does not appear for the initial celebration and then vanish. Children need to see coming to church, praying, journaling, and a host of other spiritual realties as long-term adventures. A catechist's confidence in God's ability to speak to children throughout their entire lives can be a refreshing and revolutionary point of view.

It is also important to elicit the children's own stories and help them reflect on the events of their lives. Helping children share their stories with each other and with God encourages "a living, explicit, and fruitful profession of faith (cf. *Catechism of the Catholic Church* 1229; *Christus Dominus* 14)" (GDC 66). Such reflection fosters the development of conscience and becomes the foundation for moral catechesis. Even school systems are realizing that good behavior is neither an accident nor a by-product of an entirely secular point of view. A simple way to launch children into an ongoing life-long conversation with God is to establish the practice of writing letters to Jesus in a prayer journal. A journal entry can be a way of processing a lesson. The entry can be about an episode in Scripture, an imaginary future event, or a prayer about family needs. Here is one example:

> My teacher read us the story where all the Jews went through where the water was and got away. Keep up the good work. I am Jewish. Love, Paula

In John's Gospel, Jesus says, "Before Abraham was born, 'I Am'" (Jn 8:58). Jesus is the living expression of who God is, was, and will be for our entire lives. God is timeless. When I went to Jerusalem, I found many religious places meaningful because of their geographic connection to Jesus. The Wailing Wall (a hallowed section of the biblical Temple that is revered by Jews and Christians) became an extraordinary place for me to meet God. The stone wall was a palpable sign of the never-ending presence of God, real evidence of God's boundless love. God has a passionate and immeasurable desire to be with us. The God of Abraham is eternally faithful (Ps 105:8).

Catechist's Prayer

John Henry Newman (1801–1890) was an influential Anglican scholar and clergyman in England. He participated in debates about the beliefs of Anglicans and Roman Catholics. In his pursuit of the truth he was converted to the Roman Catholic Church and later named a cardinal. He was always in favor of learning more about faith.

> God has created me to do Him some definite service;
> He has committed some work to me which he has not
>   committed to another.
> I have my mission …. I am a link in a chain, a connection
>   between persons.
> God has not created me for nothing …
> Therefore I will trust him whatever, wherever I am
> (*Novena to the Holy Spirit* 2).

Saints Who Knew How

St. Frances Cabrini (1850–1917) was an Italian-American missionary sister who endured twenty-three international ocean voyages for the sake of her ministry to immigrants. Her diary was often written, as she said, "between one wave and another." She took all these trips to bring the message of Jesus to poor immigrants, even though she was afraid of the water because she nearly drowned in a swift river when she was seven years old.

One day as an adult she told Jesus how frightened she was. Jesus promised her, "I (will) protect and guide you with my hands from one sea to the other" (*Travels of Mother Frances Xavier Cabrini* 21). After that, Frances experienced a deep and long-lasting peace. During one ocean crossing Mother Cabrini was given the nickname "sea lion" because she never became seasick. In 1912 she had a reservation to travel on the Titanic but left a month early because of an emergency at one of her hospitals. God saved her again.

Checklist For
The Aspiring Evangelist

Video stores rely on a system of categories for movies: action-adventure, sci-fi and horror, comedy, family, and new releases. Everyone has similar inner collections of personal stories. Let's browse through this inner collection. Consider starting a journal or diary to capture pieces of your own faith stories.

☐ Video store section where a movie about my life would be located

_____

☐ An event in my life that might demonstrate God's love for me

_____

☐ Someone whose faith story inspires me to believe _____

_____

☐ How often I use stories, news articles, and faith sharing during classes

_____

☐ My system for collecting "witnesses" and faith stories _____

_____

☐ How I encourage children to share budding experiences of God

_____

☐ A ten-word ad inviting children to meet God in my classes

_____

Books, Websites And Resources

Bausch, William. *Storytelling—Imagination and Faith.* Mystic, Conn.: Twenty-Third Publications, 1984. A classic for storytellers.

Bertolucci, John. *Share the Good News.* Boston: St. Paul Books and Media, 1993. Stresses ways to witness to Jesus.

Butcher, H. Maxwell. *Story As a Way to God.* San Jose, Calif.: Resource Publications, 1991. Presents some of the hows and whys of storytelling.

DeSiano, Frank, and Kenneth Boyack. *Discovering My Experience of God.* Mahwah, N.J.: Paulist Press, 1992. A workbook with reflection questions.

Finley, Mitch. *Your Family in Focus.* Notre Dame, Ind.: Ave Maria Press, 1993. Offers practical insights about growing in faith as a family.

Ghezzi, Bert. *Sharing Your Faith: a Users Guide to Evangelization.* Huntington, Ind.: Our Sunday Visitor, 1994. A helpful guide for beginners.

Hater, Rev. Robert. *News That Is Good: Evangelization for Catholics.* Notre Dame, Ind.: Ave Maria Press, 1990. Presents a clear explanation of the Gospel message.

Hoover, Brett C. *Losing Your Religion, Finding Your Faith: Spirituality for Young Adults.* New York: Paulist Press, 1998. Provides insight about the search for spirituality.

Novena to the Holy Spirit. Wheaton, Md.: The Spiritans.

Travels of Mother Frances Xavier Cabrini. Chicago: Missionary Sisters of the Sacred Heart of Jesus, 1944.

www.americancatholic.org — archive of St. Anthony Messenger Press articles, e-cards

www.cyberfaith.com presented by Sadlier — offers good links for resources

www.fea.net/bobsnook/ and *www.public.usit.net/lafpro/Kidrock/* — offer many good skits for children and adults

Something to Try: "A Peek into a Saint's Diary"

Consider helping your students keep a spiritual diary or journal. Give each student a small notebook to use as a diary and a large envelope in which to keep it. Secure the journals with string or elastic to indicate respect for the students' inner life. Promise the students that you will not read the journals when you collect them. Use sample entries from a saint's diary as examples of what to write. Invite children to listen to or read the following passages and use these headings as a guide.

1. **Something I saw. Something that happened to me.** Mother Cabrini used her time at sea to write and pray on the ship's deck. In April 1890 she wrote:

   About eleven o'clock we saw ourselves surrounded by enormous masses of ice. At first they appeared to be things of no importance, like white doves resting on the water, but afterwards, little by little, they grew much larger. They took on enormous proportions ... twelve times larger than our ship ... (like) great fortresses with cutting notches (9).

2. **God, right now I feel ...** Ask what kind of feelings might have been behind what Mother Cabrini wrote. How would she have felt? Then read her next line.

   We feel afraid of the coming night. Perhaps there will be danger.

3. **I think Jesus would answer by reminding me that ...** What do you think she wrote next? What would you write?

   We leave ourselves in the Hands of the good Jesus ... And every day we [call on Mary], the Star of the Sea, who truly protects us.

   Ask what kinds of experiences your children would write about in a journal. Then invite them to write three headings on a page in their own journals. Ask each to pick an experience from his or her own life and write about it under each heading. Remind the children to think about how they felt at the time of the experience. Ask them to add one statement that God might write back to them about the event.

Chapter Four

The Drama Of The Scriptures Comes to Life

I was in the habit of beginning each session with a procession and an enthronement of the Scriptures to help the children become aware of God's presence. After a month or two, I wanted to add a sense of the Bible's enduring importance, so I made a scroll with Isaiah 61:1–3 written on it. We read St. Luke's story (4:16–21) about Jesus reading this passage in the synagogue. I asked the children what they noticed about Jesus' attitude toward Scripture. They noticed that he believed what he read. We had a second dramatic reading of the passage with the children wearing robes and using my new scroll, which would become a regular part of our procession. We then made scrolls with dowels and tea-stained paper. Our plan was to watch and listen for meaningful Scripture passages among journal entries in the weeks ahead. Twice a year each child would pick out a favorite passage from his or her journal and copy it onto a scroll.

Voice of God and Breath of the Spirit

There are many examples of how important a few words can be—a boyfriend or girlfriend's "I love you," a doctor's diagnosis of "cancer," and practically anything that a kindergarten teacher says. We treasure certain words above all others. Catechists face the challenge of proclaiming the words of the Scriptures as rich, life-giving, and capable of touching our hearts. As a teenager, I was fortunate enough to know someone who loved the Scriptures. Ed Dolan was an elderly boarder in our home. While recovering from a bout of arthritis in his hip, he asked Mom if we had a Bible he could read. I thought he was crazy. A huge Bible with golden-edged pages lay on a table in the living room. I knew because it was my responsibility to dust it every week. Ed read it for hours at a time, and he often came looking for someone with whom to share a particular passage. His dedication to the Scriptures made me stop and think.

The *General Directory* quotes paragraph 9 of the Dogmatic Constitution on Divine Revelation (*Dei Verbum*, November 1965) when it refers to Scripture as "the speech of God as it is put down in writing under the breath of the Holy Spirit" (96). Catechists need to convey an appreciation of the Bible as both authored and enlivened by the Spirit. Think of the Spirit as hovering over us to enkindle the Scriptures in the same way that the Spirit hovers over creation and over the waters of baptism. Children, of course, are at the beginning of an appreciation of written words in general and can only begin to encounter the meaning of Scripture. Just as a small child can fall in love with a story, children of all ages can become involved in the human and spiritual dramas that are such an important part of Scripture.

St. Thérèse of Lisieux provides an interesting example of exploring the meaning of Scripture. As a teenager, she had the opportunity to visit a rich family with a new invention called an "elevator." When Thérèse prayed that evening, she looked at this amazing thing from a spiritual perspective. Therese searched the pages of the Bible looking for an "elevator" to God. She found the passage in Mark (10:16) that describes Jesus lifting small children onto his lap. His arms would be her elevators to God, she concluded. And so Thérèse's theology of the "little way" was born. St. Augustine (North Africa, 354–430) is another example of someone who was inspired and transformed through the Scriptures. In his autobiography, he describes an experience under a tree when a voice tells him to "Take and read!" When St. Augustine opened the Bible, he found a passage in Romans that said, "Let us conduct ourselves properly, as people who live in the light of day" (13:13). He then experienced a deep peace and a lasting conversion.

Scripture As the Church's Book

Not every Scripture passage is meant to be intensely meaningful, but the Scriptures are like a well that has many levels and varying depths of meaning. The *General Directory* refers to the Scriptures as the soul of cate- chesis (240). We go to the Scriptures to draw deeply of God's life. As cate- chists, we try to maintain a balance between the church's two primary stances toward the Bible. One stance is attention to context and a willing- ness to study the Bible so that you can accurately apply it as you teach. I can remember a conference speaker saying that catechists should read the entire Bible for a broader appreciation of God's word. His suggestion sounded crazy. But I took my time, skipped around a lot, and did read it all over a two-year period.

Scriptural events have many contexts, present several insights, and fit into a hierarchy of truths. The first context to consider is that the Bible is a library of different kinds of books. Another primary context is that the Bible is your textbook, which can help you maintain a focus. The *General Directory* acknowledges seven basic elements of catechesis that flow from Scripture: the Hebrew Scriptures, the life of Jesus, the history of the church, the Creed, the sacraments, the Decalogue (Ten Commandments), and the Our Father (130). Think of all these pieces of revelation as different-colored strips of sturdy fabric woven together over a year's time. These elements take turns becoming visible, but they are always entwined around each other. Each element is also like a musical instrument that offers a profound statement about the human condition and God's love. Together the elements are like an orchestra, capable of striking a resonant chord in adults and children.

The other stance toward the Bible that the church takes is a prayerful one that allows the words of Scripture to wash over us and fill us. One way to pray with Scripture is called *lectio divina* or "spiritual reading." This method has been used for centuries and is a good way to discover the levels of meaning in the Bible. First ask God to speak and imagine the Spirit's presence. Then read the text slowly in order to get an overall impression of the message. Read the text a second time and listen for a meaningful phrase, word, or image. Then write down (or circle) the phrase. Describe what the words mean for you. A young person (in fifth grade or above) would write ways in which the phrase reminds him or her of something else. A final step is to ask, "What does this say about God?"

Let's use the passage about announcing the Gospel in Romans 10:8–17. After reading it twice, I would choose verse 15, "How beautiful are the feet of those who bring good news" (New Revised Standard Version). This phrase reminds me of listening for my husband's footsteps on the porch after a long day. I want to get more excited about God speaking to me and sending me to teach.

Scripture becomes the word of God for us as we read, celebrate, and understand it together. No one person alone can grasp its meaning and importance. The Scriptures are the product of the living tradition that we celebrate in liturgy and hope to apply in many different ways. We as church pray the Scriptures through the lectionary. Years A, B, and C cover three different Gospels. During these three cycles we read almost the entire Bible except for a few small sections of a book or two. For this reason many catechists cover a passage for the upcoming Sunday liturgy so children will recognize the reading when they go to church. Unchurched children will at least be "on the same page" as the rest of the church and many other Christian denominations as well. Just saying, "We will be hearing this story again on Sunday" makes the reading part of an implicit invitation to join the community. This approach also helps children connect the Scriptures with the sacraments.

The image of the shepherd and the sheep illustrates what happens when we allow ourselves to be transformed by the Scriptures. Several shepherds often keep their flocks together in a large pen. At the end of the night they call out to their flocks, and even though the herds of sheep are large, each animal moves toward its master's voice. Then the sheep follow him to the pastures. In the same way, catechists thrive by listening to God's voice, which also forms us as a flock or faith community. God calls out to us both individually and as a community. Reading and studying the Scriptures together sharpen our spiritual ears and open our hearts so that we can follow God's voice more closely. God offers nourishment and guidance through this "living speech."

The Drama of the Bible

The Scriptures present a world rich with images and sensory appeal. Many of the stories are larger than life. Together they suggest endless variations in the ways that God relates to us. By exposing children to this world you can help them explore religious truth according to their own sensory preferences and love for the dramatic. You can use storytelling and the performing arts to help children get inside scriptural events and stories. Children can act out and redesign their faith by identifying with the main characters.

The performing arts can give an emotional voice to children's struggles with faith. Many scriptural stories have a dramatic undercurrent of belief and disbelief, such as Peter's attempt to walk on water (Mt 14:25–33) or the prophet Samuel's attempts as a boy to listen to God (1 S 3:1–11). Acting out the Scriptures helps children experience the human realities and feelings behind the drama and then apply God's revelation to their lives. At first there is almost always some grumbling and embarrassment. Characters in costumes may even wander into addressing a whole youth culture as well as their own souls. Everyone can sense that the drama may have a "*missionary dimension* rather than a strictly *catechumenal* dimension" (GDC 185). As catechists we challenge so many assumptions about life.

Useful performing arts include puppetry, mime, sign language gestures set to music, role playing, skits with props and costumes, mask drama, dance, and "live" newspaper reports. Children often feel safer acting out Bible stories if they can hide behind simple props such as an oversized shirt or fake glasses. Older children enjoy sharing their performances with younger children. An important strategy at any level is to help children get into the feelings that the people in the Scripture were experiencing. One sixth-grade class spent some time studying the Passover and the Hebrew experience of being in the desert. They discussed being lost, sunstroke, and current refugee experiences. They rewrote "Jingle Bells" as a light-hearted news spot written from a teenager's point of view.

> Dashing through the desert, without a horse or sleigh,
> O'er the sands we go, running as we pray.
> Feet and legs are sore, and slavery was a bore.
> O what fun it is to run and search for my Yahweh.
>
> Oh, jingle feet. Jingle feet. Jingle all the way.
> Oh what fun it is to run with jingle feet, Yahweh!

Another example is in a humorous novel about an unchurched family's experience of performing the Christmas pageant, called *The Best Christmas Pageant Ever* by Barbara Robinson (New York: Harper Trophy, 1988). Imogene and her brother Ralph's variation of a bedraggled Mary and Joseph looked "like the people you see on the six o'clock news—refugees, sent to wait in some strange ugly place, with all their boxes and sacks around them" (72). Everyone realized that the story was frighteningly close to the truth because "the real Holy Family [was] stuck away in a barn by people who didn't much care what happened to them." Such experiments in the presentation of Scripture set up a lively dialogue between all kinds of realities.

Promoting Gospel Values

Finally, teaching Scripture involves the third goal of evangelization outlined in *Go and Make Disciples* (a National Conference of Catholic Bishops' plan that touches every phase of parish life). We as catechists can "foster Gospel values ... promoting the dignity of the human person, the importance of the family, and the common good of society, so that our nation may continue to be transformed by the saving power of Jesus Christ" (Blum 18). As catechists we also imitate Jesus, who "made himself a *cate-chist* of the Kingdom of God for all categories of persons, great and small, rich and poor, healthy and sick, near and far, Jews and pagans, men and women, righteous and sinners, rulers and subjects, individuals and groups. … He is interested in the needs of every person, body and soul" (GDC 163).

The word of God must be addressed to the heart of our culture and take on flesh in the social and moral arenas. This is one reason for service projects. When God's word is taken seriously the boundaries between pastoral care, catechesis, evangelization, and outreach are broken down and crisscrossed over and over again. In the light of God's loving presence, people begin to see things differently. For example, the members of a Catholic parish in Littleton, Colorado, found themselves establishing a website at *saintfrancescabrini.org/* just to coordinate spiritual concerns and services to teenagers all over the country. Another example is a Massachusetts mother of a murdered teen. She found herself addressing state government officials about the death penalty. Part of what my friend Connie said was:

> I do not want our state to be internally limited by the emotions of bitterness and vindictiveness. I understand the fear one can have, but do not let fear rule. Do not become a model of murder, or an image of devaluing life …
> (I ask you this) for the sake of my grandchildren.

Another important social issue that is dear to the next generation is the state of the environment. Children are crying out for a moral ethic that respects the earth as our home and all created things as our spiritual companions. After all, Jesus was the first-born of all creation: "Through the Son, then, God decided to bring the whole universe back to himself" (Col 1:20). In *We Are Home* (Mahwah, N.J.: Paulist Press, 1993), Shannon Young describes the earth as a "conglomerate of everyday miracles. Our bodies, and the other bodies that make up the earth, are fellow travelers on this sphere as it whirls through the universe" (6). Young brings up the example of phytoplankton. Three million of them are in an ounce of seawater, and globally they remove almost one half of all the carbon dioxide in our atmosphere.

These are just a few of the many issues that children can be inspired to deal with in the light of the Gospel. They need help to sort through these issues and find a place to make a difference through the guidance of God's Spirit. You can help them grow in "a commitment to justice, according to each individual's role, vocation and circumstances (John Paul II, Encyclical Letter *Sollicitudo Rei Socialis* [December 1987], 41)" (GDC 104). You can help them begin to establish a habit of applying Gospel values to the world around them. It is the application of the Gospel that makes all the difference.

Catechist's Prayer

The *Catechism of the Catholic Church* (133) exhorts us "to learn 'the surpassing knowledge of Jesus Christ,' by frequent reading of the divine Scriptures. 'Ignorance of the Scriptures is ignorance of Christ' (*Dei Verbum* 25)." Reading and studying are meant to be lifetime habits. Begin a weekly reading time with this prayer:

> God, I hold your living word in my hands. I treasure the book of life that you have given the church. Give me a love for your Scriptures and a desire to live the Gospel. Help me recognize your voice. Send your Spirit to quicken these words and touch my heart. I believe that you have inspired these sacred writings and that you want to teach, heal, encourage, and challenge me. I ask you to open my eyes, my ears, my mind, and my heart for the sake of your children. Amen.

Saints Who Knew How

St. Ignatius of Loyola (1491–1556) was wounded while he was a Spanish soldier. During a lengthy recovery he read about Jesus and the saints. This experience changed his whole life. First he took a two-year retreat in a pauper's hospice and a cave. During this time he wrote the *Spiritual Exercises*, which outline a classic approach to Scripture. Then he founded the Society of Jesus, commonly called the Jesuits.

His steps to praying with a passage include:

1. Set the scene in your mind and ask God's help.

2. Step into the scene and look around. Choose a role to play such as the shepherd at Christmas.

3. Watch and listen for sensory details and search out the meaning of what happens in the scriptural event.

4. Identify a new insight or a resolution.

Checklist For
The Aspiring Evangelist

In a Peanuts cartoon Lucy says, "I can't help thinking that this would be a better world if everyone would listen to me." Linus answers, "Maybe we could arrange it." Her response is, "Try to get them all in one room. I hate to say things twice."

☐ Whose word, opinion, or promises do I value most?

_____

☐ What do I think and feel about reading the Bible for my own benefit?

_____

☐ What it is like for me to hear the Scripture proclaimed on Sunday?

_____

☐ In what two ways do I try to bring the Scriptures to life in my class?

_____

☐ What social or global issue would I like to bring to God?

_____

A catechist's ability to present the Gospels is related to the following qualities outlined in *Empowering Catechetical Leaders*. Rate your own efforts at achieving these goals. Give yourself a number from 1 to 5 (1 = slightly interested, 5 = very committed). Choose the item with the lowest score and think of one thing you could do to improve your efforts toward that goal.

____ I am aware that teaching is based on a unique call to serve as a messenger of the Good News. I seek ways to accept this call from God and grow in faith.

____ I want to witness to the transforming power of the Gospel. I seek God in prayer for the strength to share my faith.

____ I see myself as belonging to the People of God, especially through active membership in the local parish faith community.

____ I value the children in my care enough to pursue maturity in faith, understanding of educational methods, and mutual support among catechists.

Books, Websites
And Resources

Blum, Susan W. *Text, Study Guide & Implementation Process for Go and Make Disciples: A National Plan and Strategy for Catholic Evangelization* in the United States by the National Conference of Catholic Bishops. South Holland, Ill.: National Council of Catholic Evangelization, 1993. A study guide with questions.

A Book about Jesus. New York: American Bible Society, 1991. A young child's collection of stories translated from the New Testament in an attractive paperback format with pictures.

Costello, Elaine. *Religious Signing.* New York: Bantam Books, 1986. A dictionary. Some words are also available through an animated ASL on-line dictionary at *dww.deafworldweb.org/*

Groome, Thomas H., and Michael J. Corso, eds. *Empowering Catechetical Leaders.* Washington, D.C.: National Catholic Education Association, 1999. A scholarly collection of essays.

Martin, George. *Reading Scripture As the Word of God.* Ann Arbor, Mich.: Servant Pub, 1993. Teaches a prayerful approach to reading the Bible.

New Jerome Bible Handbook. Collegeville, Minn.: Liturgical Press, 1992.

www.catechist.com — an article archive, discussion site, catechist formation program

www.thehungersite.com — United Nations interactive site with a map of world hunger

www.pauline.org — lots of activities for kids, saint a day, teacher's guides

 ## Something to Try: "Jesus And The Storm-Tossed Boat"

Children need an active Jesus who gets involved in the details of life, a God who cares in concrete ways. Some scriptural events such as the storm on the Sea of Galilee in Mark 4:35–40 can be acted out as if they were scenes from an adventure film.

Needed: a large tablecloth (the sea) to wiggle behind the boat, 1 catechist narrator, 6 to 10 children to link arms as a boat, 2 to 4 apostles, and 1 Jesus (each with a costume item such as a hat, scarf, glasses). Read the script (a sample script follows) twice to discover the emotions, sounds, actions, and movements in the story. Add notes about these into the script.

As evening fell, Jesus and his apostles left the crowds behind and climbed into their boat. (Whoops, we need a boat. Let's start over.) Jesus was so tired that he went to the back of the boat and put his head on a cushion (*folded hands*). The apostles did a little fishing (*cast poles*) until a terrible storm whipped down through the cut in the mountains. Loud wind swirled around them. Waves began to break over the sides of the boat. Huge walls of water frightened the apostles and almost knocked them over. In a very short time the boat was full of water. The frantic apostles awakened Jesus, shouting above the wind, "Don't you care that we are drowning?" (*said by the narrator*)

Jesus got up, rubbed his eyes, and rebuked the wind. "*Be still!*" he commanded. (*Jesus speaks this part.*) The wind stopped and a great calmness filled the sea. The apostles wondered about Jesus. They didn't know what to think until one decided to thank him.

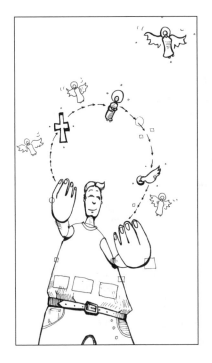

Chapter Five

Playing With The Church's Symbols

When our son Peter was nine, he didn't see the point of praying at night, and responding to all of his protests was getting tough. One night after he had put away his toys, brushed his teeth, and said good-night to Dad, I steeled my nerves for the next round of resistance. I wasn't disappointed. When I invited him to talk to Jesus, Peter exclaimed, "How can I talk to someone I can't see? How do I know if he's even here?"

As I prayed for a moment, one of those gifts of wisdom jostled my brain.

"Peter, get out of bed and I will show you that he's here," I said. We encountered my husband in the kitchen, and he was nice enough to get under the table without any explanations. The game was getting more interesting as far as Peter was concerned.

Peter and I sat down, and I asked, "Peter, is Daddy here?"

"Yeah. He's under the table."

"But I can't see him. Are you sure?" I quizzed.

"Sure I'm sure!" he giggled.

"I don't see him," I repeated.

Just then my "husband-god" reached over and tickled Peter's foot.

"Hey Dad, cut it out!"

"Peter, did you notice that you are talking to someone you can't see or hear?"

A pensive look turned into a grin, and then we all climbed under the table to pray.

We can teach children about God in innumerable ways. Every catechist with a prayer in her heart and her back to the wall finds ways. As Tess on the TV series *Touched by an Angel* said, "When your back is to the wall, you can stand up straighter." One of the biggest challenges of catechesis is bridging the distance between human experience and the God who authors the whole universe. It is difficult to help children engage in a holy dialogue between the concretes of daily life and the abstracts of God's identity. Nonetheless, the Holy Spirit helps us respond to these challenges and helps children encounter an incarnate God. One of the joys of being a catechist is dwelling in that delicious place where what we see, touch, and feel ushers us into God's presence.

What We See, Touch, Hear And Feel Can Build Faith

Children are your allies in the catechetical venture. The realm of concrete, touchable existence is their primary home. They squeeze the bread, plow through mud on bikes, and dance on the ends of their seats when it starts to snow. Only as they get older do children move from concrete reality to a transitional viewpoint and then to an ability to think in abstract terms. This is an important concept to remember because many of us are accustomed to thinking of faith as an abstract and transcendent concept. Catechists must often backtrack in order to connect faith with day-to-day events in children's lives. The surprise is that backtracking turns out to be good for us too because faith involves a tantalizing array of paradoxes, not the least of which is the immanence (closeness) and transcendence of God.

Unchurched children can discover God through a lively introduction to religious symbols, which are the sensory currency of our faith and the point contact for sacraments. "A sacramental celebration is woven from signs and symbols" (CCC 1145). The *General Directory* reminds us that when catechists teach children, they are involved in a "pedagogy of signs, where words and deeds, teaching and experience are interlinked" (143; cf. *Dei Verbum* 2). One example of this pedagogy occurred when a young ring bearer went to a Lenten wedding rehearsal. All the cactus plants and the sand in the church intrigued him. His older brother quipped, "Hey, we got a little Santa Fe going on here." The flower girl gave a brief but helpful explanation. "It's to remind us of being thirsty so we can get ready for Jesus to die on Good Friday."

Religious symbols help children explore their own powerful images. These images can sometimes be stretched to reveal spiritual realities. For example, backpacks and bikes can be used to teach because they are already invested with many levels of meaning for children. Treasured items on a prayer table can teach reverence and gratitude, a first step to counteracting rampant materialism. Your discernment of the signs and symbols in our culture can become a first step for your students in critical thinking about media, the technology of communication, and the many gods behind all of this.

At times children's personal images point toward a need for conversion in the way that a child relates to God and to the world. For example, you can help children uncover their own greed by using C. S. Lewis's description of a mentor devil's instructions to an apprentice devil in the *Screwtape Letters* (New York: Macmillan Publishing, 1961). "Even in the nursery a child can be taught to mean by 'my Teddy bear,' not the old imagined recipient of affection … but 'the bear I can pull to pieces if I like'" (98). Carl's first trip to a cemetery with a catechist aunt provides another example. He was excited about the inscriptions on the headstones, the rolling hills, and discovering his grandparents' and great-grandparents' graves.

Carl's aunt asked how he felt about being there. "After all," she said, "some people are scared of cemeteries."

"Oh, not me!" he said. "This is great. I thought dead people just got thrown out in great big trash bags."

Faith Is Uttered through Symbols

An unchurched child can be nurtured through religious images and symbols that are intimately connected to daily life. Symbols such as the cross, the bread and wine, the waters of the baptismal font, or the Bible can help a young person make physical connections with God. Symbols touch us both on the inside and on the outside, uncovering new possibilities for a flexible relationship with a tangible God. Symbols operate on the cutting edge of the interplay between right- and left-brain knowing. Imagine, for example, what a waterfall says about baptism.

Each child needs time and space to explore the meaning of a symbol on his or her own level. Fortunately, children have a natural curiosity about objects, and with some assistance can let a dynamic symbol develop in the crucible of community prayer. When children celebrate with bread and wine or with a baptismal candle, "anchoring" can take place. Powerful inner feelings thus become permanently associated with an outer reality. Children can then move from apathy or self-conscious giggling about foreign objects, such as a chalice or reconciliation room, to a shared experience of meaningful signs.

Throughout a child's faith formation, he or she needs to explore the sacraments in relation to each other and the interplay among a rich variety of symbols. A multisymbol approach allows plenty of room for God to touch children. The Holy Spirit works through many signs that become the visual and touchable jumping-off points for an encounter with God.

Children also need a multisensory approach to the many signs that will eventually come together to make one big picture of what life is about. Children are in the process of assembling this picture as they would a giant puzzle. Children watch for a dominant image for the whole of reality. Young children's drawings always include "me," "my" house, grass under "my" feet, the sky above "me," and the sun in the corner. "Me" is the dominant image. Then personal heroes emerge as "control models" for relating to the world. Marketing people capitalize on a child's tendency to adopt one character as a god, and they know how to sell that same hero as a toy, as a TV series, and as a best friend to keep that image in the child's mind for long periods of time.

You can help children keep Jesus in focus as a hero, as the "symbol of symbols" and as "the visible likeness of the invisible God" (Col 1:15). One boy, Paul, was puzzled by the idea that there are so many wafers used at a Eucharist. "Does the priest cut Jesus up into pieces?" he wanted to know. I couldn't come up with an answer, so I brought him to Father Jim. "Oh, that's simple," said the priest. "If I broke a mirror up into a hundred pieces and you looked into the broken pieces, how many Pauls would you see?" The answer was either hundreds or just one. That was the perfect image for this young boy. Jesus is both beyond physical containment yet present in places such as the unscathed tabernacle of a totally devastated church across the street from the Oklahoma bombing in 1995.

Visual Arts As a Language for Exploring The Spiritual

The visual arts can help you *present* religious symbols in ways that let children experience them on their own terms. For example, seeing several examples of what a baptismal font looks like can help children grasp the meaning of the sacrament of baptism as a bath, a swim, and a new birth. Creating visual pieces helps children bond with God through the symbol. Creating artwork provides children with thinking space and concrete ways in which to grasp the meaning of religious images. Exploring symbols through the visual arts and using these symbols when they pray brings children to God and helps them choose religious symbols as their own vehicles of faith.

Use a wealth of visual arts and techniques that foster different kinds of encounters with God. A wide variety of art activities can be suitable for several age groups. This is one area of catechesis where it helps to swap ideas and even team-teach once in a while. Here's a list of ideas to get you started:

- doodles
- paper-tearing
- clay sculpture
- banners
- potato or eraser prints
- collage

- drawing
- murals
- photos
- dioramas
- rubbings
- quilting

Find out what techniques your children are already using in school. Choose a technique that can be completed in a short amount of time or in stages over several weeks. Go for it!

One group explored what it means to touch God. They read several short Scriptures about people who touched Jesus and were healed, forgiven, or raised from the dead. Next the group mounted a piece of fabric on posterboard that represented "the hem of Jesus' robe." They used a paper-tearing technique to create a hand. They glued these reaching hands on to the robe. Finally, they closed their eyes and imagined Jesus touching them on the inside.

Formula for Using a Symbol to Teach

1. Explore the symbol physically.

Let's use ashes for our symbol. Show the children a blackened candlewick or a bowl of ashes. Ask what the ashes smell like and how it would feel in their hands.

2. Uncover related human experiences and stories.

Who has cleaned a charcoal grill or a fireplace? Who has smeared black on his or her face to play football? Who has been in a fire? (Be sure to offer sympathy and prayer for anyone who has.) During the Middle Ages children sang about the plague, "Ring around the rosy, pockets full of posies. Ashes, ashes, we all fall down." Burning things was the only way to sterilize their homes.

3. Think about the meaning of the symbol.

People in the Bible use ashes to pray about sadness. There is Daniel, who is later thrown into the lion's den (Dn 9:3), Job, and Mordecai (Es 4:1). At a much later time Jesus reads a passage from the prophet Isaiah (61:1–3) that is used to describe his mission: "to bring good news to the poor, to heal the broken-hearted ... to comfort all who mourn" (Lk 4:16–21). One translation of Isaiah goes on to say that our ashes can be replaced with wreaths of flowers—Jesus can take away sadness and bring joy.

4. Link the symbol to daily life.

Talk about one or two of the examples above and how the characters might have felt. Explain that when the priest makes the sign of the cross on our foreheads with ashes, this is a way to bring all the sadness in our hearts to Jesus. He can give us new joy and strength. Ash Wednesday and Lent help us turn toward Jesus. "Ashes, ashes, we all turn around. We turn toward you, Jesus!" could be used as a chant, a song's refrain, or a response to prayers of petition.

5. Celebrate with the symbol.

You may choose from several options depending on the age of the children. One includes writing a problem that makes us sad on a slip of paper. These pieces of paper can be burned or placed in front of a statue or candle. Signing each other on the forehead is another option. A younger group might make a picture of a sad time, then let Jesus "walk" into the picture by drawing him or by placing a sticker where he would stand.

 Catechist's Prayer

O GREAT SPIRIT, whose voice I hear in the winds and whose breath gives life to all the world, hear me! I am small and weak; I need your strength and wisdom.

Let me walk in beauty, and make my eyes ever behold the red and purple sunset.

Let my hands respect the things you have made and my ears sharp to hear your voice.

Make me wise so that I may understand the things you have taught my people.

Let me learn the lessons you have hidden in every leaf and rock. ...

Make me always ready to come to you with clean hands and straight eyes.

(Red Cloud Indian School)

Saints Who Knew How

St. Elizabeth Ann Seton (United States, 1774–1821) was a devout Protestant who always turned to the Scriptures each day as her source of guidance. She once referred to the Bible as "my book, which has spoken to me of the Most High and the Most Holy, who remains forever" (*Praying with Elizabeth Seton* 31). After her husband's death, she decided to become a Catholic. She was touched by the richness of symbols in the Catholic Church, especially the presence of Jesus in the Eucharist. She described the eucharistic bread as the "bread of angels [which] removes my pain, my cares, warms, cheers, sooths, contents and renews my whole being" (56). Her goal as a teacher was to offer a living faith that would color all of life. She founded the first Catholic parochial school in the United States. She writes about the search for God's truth wherever it is. "I often think my sins, my miseries, hide the light. Yet will I cling to my God to the last, begging for that light, and never change until I find it" (36).

Checklist For
The Aspiring Evangelist

☐ An object in the parish church that helps me experience God

_____

☐ My favorite sacrament and what its symbols mean for me

_____

☐ Objects that I use to create a prayerful atmosphere for my students

_____

☐ The most artistic quality that I have is an ability to

_____

☐ How I feel about creating works of "art" with children

_____

Checklist For
A Visual Arts Project

☐ Awaken imagination and all the senses with a description of the activity.

☐ Practice the activity with someone before class but don't bring in a finished sample. Such samples discourage creativity.

- ☐ Give clear instructions for manipulating the material **after** motivating the children about the activity.

- ☐ Provide supplies **after** the motivation and instructions.

- ☐ Comment on work. Use "Tell me about it!" not "What is it?"

- ☐ Acknowledge their accomplishments by displaying their work in a prayer corner or in a seasonal class newsletter.

Books, Websites And Resources

Alderman, Margaret, and Josephine Burns. *Praying with Elizabeth Seton.* Winona, Minn.: Saint Mary's Press, 1992.

Bausch, William. *While You Were Gone: A Handbook for Returning Catholics and Those Who Are Thinking About It.* Mystic, Conn.: Twenty Third Publications, 1994.

Cleary, William. *How the Wild Things Pray.* Leavenworth, Kans.: Forest of Peace Publishing, 1999.

Senger, Mary Cay. *Let's Learn about the Church and Celebrate Its Message.* Collegeville, Minn.: Liturgical Press, 1990. A basic textbook for children.

Snyder, Bernadette McCarver. *Did You Ever Hear a Catfish Purr?* Notre Dame, Ind.: Ave Maria Press, 1998. Offers meditations for children.

www.catholickidspages.com — games for younger kids

www.christusrex.org — religious art in Jerusalem and Rome

www.glencoe/com/benziger — activity centers, Benzi-Grr for kids

www.touched.com (site for *Touched by an Angel* television series with quotes and information

www.wctc.net/~tt/baa/ — collection of stories, poems, examples of conversion (use sparingly unless they are Jesus-centered)

Something to Try: "Lester And The Easter Secret"

This play can be used at a combined gathering of several groups, or during a Children's Liturgy of the Word. Use Act I at the beginning of Lent to introduce a stocking puppet named Lester who is a caterpillar searching for the Easter secret. Lester takes a nap on a high shelf in the vestibule at the end of Act I. He sleeps through Lent. Many families will come to Mass in order to check on him. Act II occurs right before Easter. Lester's wings are made out of two coat hangers. The construction steps are similar to the steps taken to make angel wings for Christmas. A second puppeteer is needed to operate Lester's wings. Older students can help backstage.

Props: caterpillar stocking puppet, wings, a brown "cocoon" cloth, paper flowers, handkerchief, music

Act One

Lester: Excuse me. I'm Lester and I'm lost. (*Sniffle.*) Can you help me?

Human: I'm so sorry you're lost. Let's blow your nose. Is that better?

Lester: Thank you. I feel a little better. But, but, I'm still lost. (*Cries.*) Can you help me?

Human: I can try. Where did you want to go?

Lester: My friend told me to go to St. _____ Church cause they have a "phantasmagorical" Easter secret. Yowwie! What a word! And I love secrets. So is this the right place?

Human: Well, Lester, you are at St. _____. But I'm sorry. This is Lent. We didn't get to Easter yet.

Lester: But I crawled all day. I want the secret now! Hey, all you kids, can someone point me to the Easter secret?

Human: Does anyone know what he's talking about? Does anyone know how to help? (*Take suggestions. Lester responds to various ideas but gets discouraged.*)

Lester: First, I get lost, and now no one can show me the secret! (*Sobs loudly.*)

Human: Now, Lester. (*Puts arm and blanket around caterpillar.*) I have an idea. You could snuggle up in this warm blanket and take a nice nap in the church. When you feel just a little better, peek out and whisper a prayer, just like this, "Jesus, help me. I want the Easter secret." I think something wonderful will happen. Then one of the moms will drive you home. Is that okay?

Lester: (*Sniffling.*) Okay. I am kind of tired, and this is a very comfy blanket.

(*Lester is carried out of the room.*)

"Lester and the Easter Secret" from *Evangelizing Unchurched Children* by Therese M. Boucher. © 2000 Resource Publications, Inc. All rights reserved.

The catechist invites the children to help by drawing something the caterpillar might like and by visiting the vestibule.

Act Two

Human: When I came in this morning, Lester was yawning and stretching. Let's see if he's awake. Maybe he can tell us what happened to him.

Lester: (*Yawns.*) Good morning. (*Smacking sounds.*) You're not my mommy! (*Yawns.*)

Human: It's afternoon, Lester. You took a very long nap upstairs in the church. Don't you remember?

Lester: Yes. Yes, and I woke up inside of a wonderful dream. Jesus was standing right beside me. He reached over and touched my head. Hey! I can still feel his hand. Maybe it wasn't dream. I feel all shiny inside. I think the Easter secret went all through me.

Human: What was it? What is the secret? All of us want to know, Lester. Did you see bunnies or dancing colored eggs? (*Lester: No.*) Did Jesus give you a new shirt and tie? (*Lester: No.*) Did you see bright shiny lightning? (*Lester: No.*) Tell us what happened, Lester!

Lester: Let me wiggle out of this blanket, and I'll show you. Wait a minute. My feet are stuck on the bottom. (*Caterpillar lets his body drop down behind stage. Off-stage dialogue.*) Come on, foot. That's it. Come on, legs. Come on, toes. Wow! This is great! I've got it! I've got it! Thank you, Jesus.

Human: (*To children.*) What do you think is happening?

Lester: (*Appears as butterfly.*) The Easter secret is new life! Jesus gave me new life. I found the biggest, best secret of all. Yeah! Let's celebrate with a song.

Human: We can sing with you. Just lead us.

All: (*Sing "New Life" or other suitable tune.*)

Human: This is exciting. I'm so happy for you, Lester. I hope Jesus can do something like this for all of us, too. Oh, I'll find a mom to give you a ride home so you can show your family.

Lester: Thanks anyway, but I'm flying home. Thanks for everything. Happy Easter! Bye, everybody!

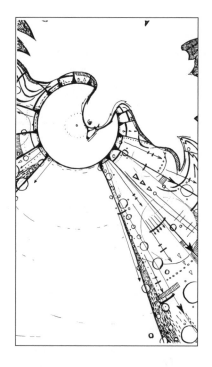

Chapter Six

What More Can An Evangelist Do?

Rose was sitting in my office with a complaint about a preschool Christmas assignment that her daughter Michelle had brought home. It was a drawing of the gifts that God had given.

"God didn't give Michelle anything for Christmas," Rose insisted. "My husband did. He worked two jobs to give her all this!" she said as she glared and pointed at the toys in the drawing.

"Well," I began with caution. "Let's imagine that you are Michelle and that you were asked to draw things that you are thankful for during the Christmas season. What would you draw?" I asked.

Rose thought for a moment. "I'm thankful for good health. Lots of our friends are sick right now."

"And how about your husband?" I asked. "Is he well?"

"Yes, he is, especially compared to last year when he kept getting strep."

"Do you suppose that in some strange way we could say that God gave your husband good health this year and that meant he could work and buy more gifts? Could this mean that in some remote way God brought those toys to Michelle?"

"Why, yes. When you put it that way, it's true. Thanks. Oh, and by the way, is it okay if this month's tuition is a week late?"

As I stepped back from my conversation with Rose, I faced an ever-growing dilemma that catechists deal with daily. How can we offer children a living faith that will endure any other influences? How can catechists reach children's families so that what happens in the classroom is not "wasted"? After all, catechists have only a few short hours of contact with the youngest members of a family. Can catechists help convey the message of the Gospel to everyone whom parish religious education programs touch?

Essential Moments of Evangelization

This would be a good time to summarize what we have already discussed. Inactive or unchurched families send their children to us for instruction, formation, and character development or for the sake of family politics and to stay in touch with a spiritual organization. Some don't even know why they send their children. Catechists must respect these reasons but look beyond the surface. God sends these children. You are called to stir up the baptismal waters given in infancy so that these children can experience the life-giving springs of God's love. You are preparing them for a time when they can decide to unleash these waters for themselves as adult believers. You are a guide along one small part of the journey. More guides will share their lives as followers of Jesus and members of the Body of Christ. On a good day you know that Jesus is present as a master catechist and will give these children glimpses of his presence in their homes and families. Faith is not a matter of making a long-distance phone call, sending a satellite signal, waiting for a website that is under construction, or overcoming a maze of obstacles. God is accessible to these children twenty-four hours a day.

Evangelizing children does not necessarily mean adding to your lessons, although that may happen. You must take a sharper focus and present an unfolding invitation to come and see what God wants to give them through the church. You can introduce the church's treasures—stories of faith, the sacramental touch of Jesus, the creeds that we profess, the voice of God in Scripture, the call to act out Gospel values, and the touch of God through religious symbols. Because of the high percentage of unchurched children, it is important to stress a life-long invitation to faith as a gift that is freely given.

Some catechists, such as my friend Mary in Chapter Three, discover that teaching children about God becomes an "essential moment" in their own journeys toward God. Just hearing the message of God's love and translating that love into everyday language becomes its own invitation and challenge. If this is happening to you, then find support for your own growth as an adult disciple. You might start with courses offered in your parish or at a nearby retreat center. Another option is exploring one of many renewal movements such as Renew, Cursillo, charismatic renewal, Disciples in Mission, or Teams of Our Lady. These can be located with the help of parish or diocesan offices.

Build Disciples and a Culture of Belief

You can offer children a chance to grow a few steps closer to God and a place to bring concerns about the needs of the whole family. In some cases children will become "refrigerator evangelists" through the pictures, prayers, stories and artwork they display. In addition to this indirect contact with families, we can help design parent meetings, letters, projects, and celebrations that are sensitive but deliberate opportunities for parents to meet God in a new way. One catechist involves his children in making a "family of faith" tablecloth that includes small pictures of Jesus, the apostles, and the children in the class at the Last Supper. The tablecloth travels from home to home for the rest of the year. Family members add their names near the pictures of their children.

The formation that you offer children is an apprenticeship in the entire Christian life (GDC 67). You can offer several tools such as journaling and praying for their families. Your lessons might help the children discover God in the sacrificial love of a movie character, in episodes from the lives of current saints, or in religious symbols. You can bolster confidence in the good that is around them. Even though it is difficult for children to be overt about their beliefs or to share with their peers, you can provide them with spiritual affirmation, a safe place for reflection, and the evangelistic nourishment that is an important part of their growth in faith. You can equip children with religious language and prepare them for future conversations about God with a parent, relative, or neighbor.

Evangelizing beyond Class Time

Your own baptismal identity as a Catholic involves a call to share the Gospel with even more people. Faith sharing and evangelization are meant to be parts of daily life. The document called *Go and Make Disciples* offers us ways to answer this call. The first way is to live with "such an enthusiasm for [your] faith that, in living [your] faith in Jesus, [you] freely share it with others" (24).

A young man, hoping for one final word that would last a lifetime, approached his dying father in a hospital. As the young man leaned over his father to listen, the dying man said, "Paul, promise me that you will make something of yourself." In much the same way, the last words of Jesus were, "Go and make disciples" (cf. Mt 28:19). Realizing the first goal of evangelization involves asking, "Am I making a disciple of myself for the sake of the Gospel?" The values, dreams, and goals that you embody have an effect on those around you. If the Good News is at the core of your being, then "Such a witness is already a silent proclamation of the Good News and a very powerful and effective one. Here we have an initial act of evangelization" and a basis for authentic sharing with others (Pope Paul IV, *On Evangelization in the Modern World*, 21).

Evangelization also involves a willingness to verbalize your faith in God as a response to people's spiritual needs. Ask yourself, "Do I freely share my faith?" Sharing faith stories is not a "them and us" or a "have and have not" proposition but a realization of a common need for God. Evangelization is "one blind beggar showing another blind beggar where the bread is" (an anonymous definition). Another part of sharing our faith involves "inviting all people … whatever their social or cultural background, to hear the message of salvation in Jesus Christ so that they may come to join us in the fullness of the Catholic faith" (*Go and Make Disciples* 26). This mission means offering open-ended support and invitations to parish events. At this point you may be thinking, "It is enough of a challenge to try this kind of sharing with children. How could I possibly do this with peers?" You may wonder, "How can I make disciples when I can barely follow Jesus myself?" We all have these same misgivings. When asked to what religious group he belonged, C. S. Lewis once replied, "I am a lapsed atheist."

Radical Dependence on the Spirit

Your success in evangelizing others is possible when you begin with a radical openness to the Holy Spirit. God wants to use all of us to answer the needs of those around us—physical, economic, social, and even spiritual needs. As a catechist you have experience talking about God and a growing sensitivity to the spiritual needs of others. You can be an instrument of the compassion of Jesus and the passionate fire of the Holy Spirit. Catechists can set spiritual fires. In her diary St. Frances Cabrini reminds us that the Spirit "will come and penetrate into the very center of your heart, purifying it, changing it, enlightening it, consuming it with the flames of holy and divine love" (*Travels of Mother Frances Xavier Cabrini* 80).

For about a century people believed that all forest fires were bad. Chief Jack Ward Thomas of the U.S. Forest Service explained the situation in *Parade Magazine* (22 September 1996):

> We thought we could control fire indefinitely, but we were wrong. Now we have to return fire to our forests deliberately …. Fire is an important part of the ecology of our forests. It prunes out old, sick trees and plants. Only the intense heat of a forest fire causes certain trees to germinate and grow. Idle

carelessness is still undesirable, but forests actually need "prescribed fires" the way people may need medicine or discipline.

So, too, some of your children, their families, neighbors, and fellow parishioners need a real spiritual fire in order to come to faith. Some need warm, intimate encounters that are like cuddling up to a fireplace on a cold day. Some need energizing fires like the burning bush that Moses encountered. Many need "prescribed fires" to release the raw energy and transformation of the Spirit of God. We all need the steady fire of the Spirit like the earth needs the sun for warmth, food production, daylight, and weather stability. Spiritual renewal is part of life itself. Think of the traditional prayer that begins with "Come, Holy Spirit, fill the hearts of your faithful and kindle in them the fire of your love. Send forth your Spirit and they shall be created and you will renew the face of the earth." Pray with the Carmelite St. Mary Magdalen dei Pazzi (Italy, 1566–1607), who called on the Spirit to "consume in us whatever prevents us from being consumed in You" (*Prayer Book of the Saints* 139).

Most important for us as catechists are children who need entire parishes that are on fire with God's love in a visible and palpable way and communities in which every kind of evangelization is taking place. When we look at how the Spirit ignited the gift of faith in our lives, we can usually recall the witness of several individuals. For me, it was Mom who invited me to go to weekday Mass during Lent; my grandmother who gave me a book about the saints; Ray, who directed the children's choir; and Dad, who became one of the first deacons in our diocese. Dad's life-long desire to see his children come back to church is still inspiring. In the last few moments before a recent surgery, he quickly dismissed my desire to pray for him. Instead, he wanted to pray for each son or daughter by name, stopping to ask God to bring each unchurched "child" back. I thank God for all of these evangelists who helped me choose God.

During the dozens of workshops that I have given about evangelization, I always ask how many have a loved one who has stopped going to church. Every hand goes up. It is the aching hearts behind these hands to which you can respond as an evangelizing catechist. These people are praying for you. You are not alone in your efforts. You are part of the Body of Christ, the communion of saints, the People of God. If you listen carefully, you can hear their faith echoed in St. Paul's prayer:

> [I] ask the God of our Lord Jesus Christ, the glorious Father, to give you the Spirit who will make you wise and reveal God to you .... I ask that your minds be opened to see his light, so that you will know what is the hope to

which he has called you, how rich are the wonderful blessings he promises
to his people, and how very great is his power at work in us who believe.
This power working in us is the same as the mighty strength which he used
when he raised Christ from death (Eph 1:15–21).

Catechists As Prophets of an Evangelistic Vision

In previous generations, evangelization happened almost by osmosis—from
one generation to another, from one friend or schoolmate to another. Now
that these links are under more stress, we must consider deliberate
evangelization. St. Paul is speaking to us when he says, "do the work of an
evangelist" (2 Tim 4:5, NRSV). Together, we have a tremendous opportunity to step in and forge new and vital connections with children, their
families, and the people in our daily lives. There is always more of Jesus to
share with others. A good way to think of evangelization is in term of the
groupings of people with whom we share Jesus—small-group, one-to-one,
or large-group evangelization.

You are probably most familiar with small-group evangelization, which
can include children's catechetical sessions, Renew groups, Scripture study
groups, and small faith sharing groups. Even grade-level catechist meetings
can become a support for evangelization when the elements of prayer,
study, and faith sharing are added to the agenda of the meeting. Every
family is meant to be a small faith community in which the presence of Jesus
binds the members together. I met a man who was heartbroken about his
grandson Brian. The young man had been buying drugs and was arrested
the day before his grandpa's birthday. The family party was subdued at best.
Just as the boy's mother prepared to fetch the birthday cake, Grandpa
placed a brown bag in the middle of the dining room table.

"Just a minute," he said. "We have something else to do first."

He took out a statue of Mary and announced, "We are going to pray the
rosary just like we did when some of you were kids. And we're going to pray
for Brian." It was an important moment for everyone. They were able to
give their pain and grief to God through Grandpa's simple but honest invitation to share their faith.

You can also share or pray with someone in need on a one-to-one basis.
You can take a moment to pray with a child who bursts into the room with
happy news or with deep concern about a family tragedy. Your responses
can be just a few short words addressed to God. Evangelization also involves
either informal or deliberate one-to-one faith sharing and can be structured
around a religious education program. Some catechists make an effort to get
to know parents informally. Some parishes interview families as part of the

sacramental preparation process. Others provide teams of parents who visit families involved in direct preparation for first communion. Some parishes offer drop-in centers for parents during their children's classes. In the case of unchurched families, catechists often function as hospitality ministers on behalf of the larger parish. Of course, we can't assume that parents want to talk about God, but on the other hand, we can watch for individual parents who are ready to grow in faith and are open to sharing.

Your awareness of the large numbers of inactive families participating in parish programs is not meant to be a source of discouragement. We are called to a prophetic "*passion for renewal in the ministry of adult faith formation* ... relying on the grace of the Holy Spirit." We can advocate for parent programming with a genuine conviction that we need "*a comprehensive, multi-faceted, and coordinated approach* to adult faith formation" (*Our Hearts Were Burning Within Us: A Pastoral Plan for Adult Faith Formation in the United States* [NCCB/USCC, 1999], 7, 34).

The third kind of evangelization is directed at large groups and includes events such as Christmas pageants, Ash Wednesday services, and what is called "project evangelization." Project evangelization presupposes a willingness to develop an "evangelistic" dimension for some parish liturgies. Of course, any big project involves the support of parish staff, training in evangelization, and a lot of work. The advantage of choosing project evangelization is that it can galvanize efforts to reach out to inactive Catholics and expose parishioners to the vision behind evangelization. Many fine options for project evangelization are listed at the end of this chapter.

I have worked with several parishes who have used the Ashes to Fire program. Ash Wednesday certainly involves large crowds of people, but the liturgies in the average parish are not usually designed to reach out to inactive Catholics. This project incorporates insights that were discovered in offering Catholic follow-up to a Billy Graham Crusade in our diocese. At St. Elizabeth's we designed several Ash Wednesday services that included a short witness describing the importance of Jesus in an individual's life. One of the leaders of the Moms and Tots Group shared her story and invited several group members to come for moral support. Not only did they come but many also returned to regular attendance at Mass.

Many small acts of evangelization involve displaying children's visual and literary pieces in parish space or in the bulletin. During May, one parish created a large vase for Mary with paper flowers made by first communion candidates. More possibilities surface when we consider using the performing arts in conjunction with liturgies, festivals, and social events that are already in place. The use of performing arts in the context of the adult faith community helps children feel at home and can help adults grasp the Gospel message in a simple and direct manner. A bazaar or potluck supper might include a booth featuring puppet shows, a religious film festival, or a play about the parish's history. Seasonal events such as a Christmas tree lighting or an Easter egg hunt might include a few children's poems and a parent's two-minute witness. There are hundreds of ways to let the message of God's love take flesh among us. There are thousands of ways to foster spiritual growth and vitality among us. As Teilhard de Chardin once said in the *Hymn of the Universe* (New York: Harper and Row Publishers, 1961),

> The Incarnation means the renewal, the restoration, of all the energies and powers of the universe; Christ is the instrument, the Centre and the End of all creation, animate *and* material; through him everything is created, hallowed, quickened (144).

Will you let yourself become a part of this restoration? Will you offer your voice as storyteller, your insights into Scripture, your lesson plans—in short, all of your efforts as a catechist—to God for the sake of the Gospel? Will you offer both your gifts and your limitations to the great enterprise of making disciples? I am reminded of an old story about a rather plain and uninteresting priest who prayed that people would be converted through his homilies. He wanted to do so much more. One Friday night Father Crachet spent hours in prayer and came up with an inspiring homily. He wrote it all down so he wouldn't leave out a single word. That Sunday's sermon went well as far as he was concerned, except for the time when he lost his place. Father cleared his throat and made a remark about turning the page. Later in the vestibule a man thanked him for his inspiring message. "What part of the homily struck you?" Father Crachet asked. (By the way, this is a very important question to ask after any catechetical session. Now back to our priest.) The man shifted from one foot to the other in embarrassment and answered, "It was when you said, 'And now we must turn the page!' That's just what I need to do with my life. Thank you."

The coming of the third millennium provides us with an occasion for learning more about Catholic evangelization. Pope John Paul II dedicated the last decade of the twentieth century to a new evangelization that will bring "a new springtime" to the church. We, as church, "must increase our apostolic zeal to pass on to others the light and joy of the faith" (*Mission of the Redeemer* 86). Even though we may associate evangelization with "Bible preachers" and door-to-door visits by religious sects, we need to reclaim evangelization as a Catholic reality. We have always made a distinction between St. John the Baptist and St. John the Evangelist. Yes, evangelization involves the Gospel. "[It] must be viewed as the process by which the Church, moved by the Spirit, proclaims and spreads the Gospel throughout the entire world" (GDC 48). For us as Catholics and as catechists, "evangelization is an essentially ecclesial act" (78). We must find ways to share faith and invite people into the Body of Christ.

Catechist's Prayer

The bishops of the United States ended their document on evangelization, *Go and Make Disciples*, with this prayer (22). Let us join them.

> We pray that [we as] Catholic people will be set ablaze with a desire to live [our] faith fully and share it freely with others.
> May [our] eagerness to share faith bring a transformation to our nation …. We pray that the fire of Jesus enkindled in us by God's Spirit may lead more and more people in our land to become disciples, formed in the image of Christ our Savior. Amen.

Saints Who Knew How

Blessed Peter To Rot (1912–1945) was the son of a chief in Rakunai, New Britain, off the coast of Papua, New Guinea. He was one of the first converts on this remote island and became a full-time catechist at age eighteen. He prepared people for sacraments and sought out people who were most in need of conversion. After three years in this mission, he married Paula la Varpit, and they built a family life centered on Jesus. He often did something unheard of in his culture by asking his wife's forgiveness for his failings.

Peter's life and ministry became intolerable with the Japanese invasions of World War II. All the missionary priests were imprisoned. Religious activities were banned. The conversion of the whole island was challenged through the legalization of polygamy. At first, Peter went quietly among the villages as a catechist sustaining the people's faith. After a while, he found it necessary to use an underground shelter in order to baptize and teach. He often taught about the holiness of marriage. When he denounced a Japanese official who had two wives, Peter was arrested, imprisoned, and martyred. His last words to his wife were, "Do not worry. I am a catechist, and I am only doing my duty." He was beatified in 1995.

Checklist for The Aspiring Evangelist

St. Cyril of Jerusalem (315–386) describes the Spirit as a light that floods the soul and explains, "The Spirit comes with the tenderness of a true friend and protector to save, to heal, to teach, to counsel, to strengthen, to console. The Spirit comes to enlighten the mind first of the one who receives Him and then, through Him, the minds of others as well" (*Novena to the Holy Spirit* 17). It is important to look at how we as believers and as catechists cooperate with the Spirit in proclaiming the Gospel.

- ☐ My favorite image for the Holy Spirit: Paraclete, Breath of God, Wind, Living Flame, Dove, Seat of Wisdom, Spirit of Truth, Spirit of Christ _____

- ☐ I seek the inspiration of the Spirit for myself and as a catechist by _____

- ☐ Something I am doing to "perform the work of an evangelist" is _____

- ☐ One way I share the struggles of evangelizing children with other catechists is to _____

- ☐ Something I will do to learn more about evangelization is _____

- ☐ How I convey the importance of the Gospel for the entire world _____

 ## Books, Websites And Resources

Aridas, Chris, Stephen Benthal, and John Boucher. From Ashes to Fire: A Parish Process for Lenten, Eastertime, and Pentecost Evangelization. Brentwood, New York: CHARISM, 1999. See *www.drvc.com.* An information booklet is available at CHARISM, PO Box 1301, Brentwood, NY 11717 or (631) 952-7517 or through e-mail: *jjbcharism@aol.com.*

Blum-Gerding, Susan. *Heart to Heart Evangelization: Building Bridges between Proclamation and Justice.* Bluffton, S.C.: Jeremiah Press, Inc., 1996–97. Isaiah Missions, Inc., e-mail: *ismission@aol.com.* A workbook and facilitator's guide for parish-based training.

Blum-Gerding, Susan, and Frank P. DeSiano. *Lay Ministers, Lay Disciples—Evangelizing Power in the Parish.* New York: Paulist Press, 1999. Presents a refreshing vision for each parish ministry.

Dollen, Charles, ed. *Prayer Book of the Saints.* Huntington, Ind.: Our Sunday Visitor, 1984.

Kemps, Carrie, and Donald Pologruto. *Catholics Coming Home: A Journey of Reconciliation for Churches Reaching Out to Inactive Catholics.* New York: Harper Collins, 1991. A book that assists ministry to inactive Catholics using storytelling and materials that can be duplicated.

Novena to the Holy Spirit. Wheaton, Md.: The Spiritans.

www.catholic.org — saints, daily readings, Scripture search, many links

www.catholicevangelization.org/ — National Council for Catholic Evangelization (NCCE)

www.paulist.org/pncea — Paulist National Catholic Evangelization Association — can also be reached at (202) 832-5022—features include "Meet a Catholic Evangelizer"

 ## Something to Try: "Finding Jesus In Our Community (Collected Interviews)"

Invite the children to ask two or three people (extended family members or adult friends) about what it means to believe in God. Provide the children with questionnaires that include a short introduction. You might also give them the names of one or two parishioners whom you have recruited ahead of time for a telephone interview. Compile the answers to the questionnaire as a group and print copies for everyone who has helped. Below are sample introduction and questions:

My name is _____. My religion class is curious about what it means to believe in God. We need to know what you think. Any answer you give will help us. There are no wrong answers as far as we are concerned. We are going to share your answers in our class, but I will not give anyone your name if you so choose. Will you answer these questions for us?

What was church like when you were my age? Who taught you about Jesus?

What sacraments have you received? Name a good thing about one of them.

What do you think about the Bible? Why would someone want to read it?

One important thing to remember about God is _____.

Extra questions for family members: Were you at my baptism? What was it like?

A more involved project for older children entails helping a family member write a brief personal history or a recollection of several inspiring or powerful events. Many tips for such a project are at the Center for Life Stories Preservation, *www.storypreservation.com*, 137 Bates Ave., St. Paul, MN 55106, telephone (612) 774-5016 and at the "My History is America's History" website (*www.myhistory.org/*), which is sponsored by the National Endowment for the Humanities.

Glossary of Terms

catechesis: Teaching what God has revealed especially in Jesus and transmitting the church's lived experience of the Gospel so that others may appropriate it and profess it. "The aim of catechetical activity consists in precisely this: to encourage a living, explicit and fruitful profession of faith" (*General Directory for Catechesis* 66; see also *Catechism of the Catholic Church* 1229 and *Christus Dominus* 14).

catechumenate: A time of formal preparation for initiation into the church, which involves formation, worship, community life, study, and certain rites. The whole process is sometimes called "being in the RCIA," which stands for *Rite of Christian Initiation of Adults*. A recent pope referred to adults who have celebrated the sacraments of initiation (baptism, confirmation, and Eucharist) without any significant conversion as "quasi-catechumens."

conversion: A change of heart or transformation in our lives, either as individuals or as a society. A movement toward God that comes about through the power of the Holy Spirit. Conversion involves a continuous process that occurs in the emotional, intellectual, moral, and social areas of life.

evangelization: In *Go and Make Disciples* an earlier definition by Pope Paul VI is paraphrased—"bringing the Good News of Jesus into every human situation and seeking to convert individuals and society by the divine power of the Gospel itself" (2; cf. *Evangelii Nuntiandi* 18). It includes both the proclamation of Jesus and the "response of the person in faith, both being the work of the Spirit of God" (10).

inactive Catholic: Someone who identifies himself or herself as Catholic but goes to Sunday liturgies less than twice in six months, not counting Christmas, Easter, weddings, and funerals. Estimates are that this includes seventeen to eighteen million people in the United States.

religious symbols: Emotionally and spiritually charged objects, images, words, or gestures. Revelation is mediated through symbols with many levels of meaning. A symbol is a radiant node, a vortex, a "powerful Epiphany of all its meanings at once" (Robert Farrar Capon, *Hunting the Divine Fox* [New York: Seabury Press, 1974]).

unchurched: Someone who does not identify with any church and "who has not voluntarily worshipped in *any church*, synagogue, or temple within the past six months other than for high holy days, Christmas, Easter, weddings or funerals." This includes about sixty to eighty million Americans or 44 percent of the population (George Gallup, *The Unchurched American* [1988] and Paulist National Catholic Evangelization Association [1999]).

witness: To give credibility to what you believe by living a life that reflects God's love. To share faith stories—descriptions of events that have helped you recognize God's presence in day-to-day life. To offer a brief summary of what Jesus means in the context of one's whole life.